More Praise for *The 8 Dimensions of Leadership*

"For a fresh outlook on what it takes to be a great leader, read this book. *The 8 Dimensions of Leadership* is an insightful, practical guide—a leader could spend ten or twenty years learning some of the lessons you'll take away. Don't wait."

—Keith Ferrazzi, bestselling author of *Never Eat Alone*

"*The 8 Dimensions of Leadership* is a treasure trove of practical leadership advice. Built upon a solid research-based foundation, the book is a remarkable collection of proven developmental strategies. Clear and engaging, it is a must-read for those who aim to sharpen their leadership skills and improve their interpersonal effectiveness."

—Steven Snyder, founder and Managing Director, Snyder Leadership Group, and former CEO, Net Perceptions Inc.

"It is always refreshing to read a research-based book on leadership that presents convincing evidence that the best leaders are not 'single celled' or 'one-trick ponies.' The book guides all leaders to discovering new behaviors that enable them to go beyond their autopilot approaches and the ultimate ruts that so many leaders dig for themselves."

—Jack Zenger, CEO, Zenger Folkman, and coauthor of the bestselling *The Extraordinary Leader* and *The Extraordinary Coach*

"The quest for leadership is first an inner quest to discover who you are, and one of the best places to begin that quest is with *The 8 Dimensions of Leadership*. Jeffrey Sugerman, Mark Scullard, and Emma Wilhelm challenge the widely accepted, but fundamentally flawed, assumption that you should lead only with your strengths. They argue most persuasively that you must stretch yourself beyond your primary dimension in order to meet the demands of today's multidimensional environment. This highly personalized book is based on solid evidence, crammed with real-life examples, and full of practical suggestions that you can use immediately. You will be, as I was, richly rewarded when you read it and apply it."

—Jim Kouzes, Dean's Executive Professor of Leadership, Leavey School of Business, and coauthor of the bestselling *The Leadership Challenge* and *The Truth about Leadership*

"An enormously valuable book for anyone interested in greater effectiveness in the new era of leveraging relationships! So much of what many of us want to get done these days requires an understanding of what makes us more or less comfortable as we engage with our world and the key people in it, and this should be considered a prime resource. Don't let the simplicity and easily intuitive quality of its contents fool you. This is a power tool. As a more than twenty-year DiSC profile user and advocate, I was already familiar with and sympathetic to the basic model. But as I engaged with its simple but subtle concepts and suggestions, I was stunned by its ability to hit home for me in so many aspects of my own current leadership challenges and opportunities. It delivered instant validation and inspired direction for me. Bravo!"

—**David Allen, Chairman, David Allen Company, and author of** *Getting Things Done*

The 8 Dimensions of Leadership

The 8 Dimensions of Leadership:

DiSC® Strategies for Becoming a Better Leader

Jeffrey Sugerman
Mark Scullard
Emma Wilhelm

BK

Berrett–Koehler Publishers, Inc.
San Francisco
a BK Business book

Berrett-Koehler Publishers, Inc.
235 Montgomery Street, Suite 650
San Francisco, CA 94104-2916
Tel: (415) 288-0260   Fax: (415) 362-2512   www.bkconnection.com

Ordering Information

Quantity sales. Special discounts are available on quantity purchases by corporations, associations, and others. For details, contact the "Special Sales Department" at the Berrett-Koehler address above.

Individual sales. Berrett-Koehler publications are available through most bookstores. They can also be ordered directly from Berrett-Koehler: Tel: (800) 929-2929; Fax: (802) 864-7626; www.bkconnection.com

Orders for college textbook/course adoption use. Please contact Berrett-Koehler: Tel: (800) 929-2929; Fax: (802) 864-7626.

Orders by U.S. trade bookstores and wholesalers. Please contact Ingram Publisher Services, Tel: (800) 509-4887; Fax: (800) 838-1149; E-mail: customer.service@ ingrampublisherservices.com; or visit www.ingrampublisherservices.com/Ordering for details about electronic ordering.

Berrett-Koehler and the BK logo are registered trademarks of Berrett-Koehler Publishers, Inc.

Printed in the United States of America

Berrett-Koehler books are printed on long-lasting acid-free paper. When it is available, we choose paper that has been manufactured by environmentally responsible processes. These may include using trees grown in sustainable forests, incorporating recycled paper, minimizing chlorine in bleaching, or recycling the energy produced at the paper mill.

Library of Congress Cataloging-in-Publication Data

Sugerman, Jeffrey.
The 8 dimensions of leadership : DiSC strategies for becoming a
better leader / Jeffrey Sugerman, Mark Scullard, Emma Wilhelm.
   p. cm. -- (Bk business)
Includes index.
ISBN 978-1-60509-955-2 (pbk. : acid-free paper)
1. Leadership. I. Scullard, Mark. II. Wilhelm, Emma. III. Title.
IV. Title: Eight dimensions of leadership. V. Series.

BF637.L4S875 2011
658.4'092--dc22   2011007600

First Edition
16 15 14 13   10 9 8 7 6

Book Producer & Designer—Jimmie Young/Tolman Creek Media. Copy Editor—Sarah Tannehill. Indexer—Shan Young. Cover Design—Irene Morris. Cover Image—Don Bishop/Getty Images. Author Photos—Paul Markert, www.markertphoto.com.

Dedication

To the 1800 members of the Inscape Network, the most extraordinary collection of trainers, consultants, coaches, and entrepreneurs that could ever be imagined. We could not do this work without you. Thank you for your trust and confidence in the Inscape Team.

Contents

Preface

This book is about broadening your definition of what constitutes effective leadership. As we interviewed senior executives and listened to their reactions to the lessons in the book, we frequently heard, "I wish I'd heard these earlier in my career." We hope that this book can accelerate your leadership development by removing some of the serendipity that is often required to learn important life lessons. We also hope that you will gain a sense of freedom with respect to your role as a leader—an understanding that you are not trapped in your current leadership style. In fact, you have the power to choose alternative ways of thinking, acting, and behaving in the leadership activities you are responsible for today.

Why should you broaden your definition of leadership? In the current climate of intense economic and political uncertainty, many thought leaders conceptualize effective organizational leadership in terms of driving mission clarity, precise strategy execution, and management of extremely complex systems. And without a doubt, these competencies are crucial for leaders in the 21st century. At the same time, we have found that there are consistent demands on leaders to demonstrate greater flexibility in how they respond to rapidly fluctuating circumstances.

Peter F. Drucker described these demands succinctly: "[Leaders] require the capacity to analyze, to think, to weigh alternatives, and to harmonize dissent. But they also require the capacity for quick and decisive action, for boldness and for intuitive courage. They require being at home with abstract ideas, concepts, calculations and figures. They also require perception of people, a human awareness, empathy, and all together a lively interest in people and respect for them." The purpose of this book is to provide leaders at all levels with a straightforward method to understand their personal leadership equations, and more importantly, a model to increase their flexibility in navigating beyond their comfort zones of leadership behavior. We believe that multidimensional leaders are more effective in responding to rapidly shifting circumstances than leaders who cling to what they do best.

The 8 Dimensions of Leadership is based on the DiSC® model of human behavior, a system of psychology that helps explain how "normal" people think, feel, and act based on the dynamic interplay of four major emotional reactions: Dominance, Influence, Steadiness, and Conscientiousness. The concepts behind DiSC® were articulated in the 1920s by Dr. William Moulton Marston, formalized and commercialized in the 1970s by Dr. John Geier, and further advanced by the Inscape Publishing research team.

In Part 1 of the book, we introduce you to the 8 Dimensions of Leadership—a DiSC-based typology of leadership styles—and provide access to an online assessment to help you determine your primary leadership dimension. In Part 2, we explore the common psychological drivers associated with each of the eight dimensions. In Part 3, we help you determine what lessons from the eight dimensions might be most relevant to your leadership development at this point in your career. We then provide a set of lessons and suggestions to help you increase your flexibility in the dimensions you choose to work on. We don't expect you to read Part 2 and Part 3 of the book end-to-end. Instead, we suggest that you read the chapters that are most relevant to you and come back to the book when circumstances demand a change in your leadership style.

Acknowledgements

We have the good fortune of being part of an organization that has the rare ability to function in the true sense of a high-performing team. This book would not have been possible without the support of the entire Inscape Publishing organization, especially Barry Davis, Susie Kukkonen, Julie Straw, Jidana James, Lisa Payne, Brad Meyer, Rachel Broviak, and Tracy LaChance.

We also spent time interviewing leaders in various organizations to help validate research findings and bring the data to life. We thank Michael Berman, Steven A. Carples, Genevra Cusic, Bettina Sawhill Espe, Ryan Foss, Don Hudson, Erin Matson, Sam Richardson, Darrell Thompson, Wendy A. Wade, Ph.D., and Carol Watson, along with several who wish to be unnamed, for the time, effort, and wisdom they brought to our conversations about life as a leader. The staff of Berrett-Koehler added tremendous value to this book. Every author should be lucky enough to work with a team of professionals who have not lost the art of great editing, design, and development of a manuscript. Special thanks to Steve Piersanti (Resolute leader) who challenged us to develop our ideas and express them clearly; Jeevan Sivasubramaniam, who kept a messy process moving smoothly; the entire BK staff, especially Michael Crowley, David Marshall, Dianne Platner, Cynthia Shannon, Rick Wilson, and Jimmie Young; as well as the Berrett-Koehler reviewers, who helped us make some significant improvements between versions.

Each of the authors would also like to acknowledge some special people who have helped to make this project possible. Jeffrey would like to thank Sarah Schultz for her love and support. Mark would like to thank Jill Scullard for being such a generous and accepting wife and friend. Emma would like to thank Josh Wilhelm, Pete Sandberg, and the many friends who provided support and valuable feedback. She would also like to thank Leslie Sandberg, Rose Wilhelm, and Elizabeth Paro for making it possible for her to be a successful professional *and* parent.

Part 1
The 8 Dimensions of Leadership Model

*T*he *8 Dimensions of Leadership* is meant to provide a highly personalized leadership development experience. Part 1 helps you get the most out of the book by providing important background information on DiSC®, describing the 8 Dimensions of Leadership, and explaining the value of this multidimensional model. In essence, you'll get a big-picture sense of how this model can help you bypass some of the trial and error often involved in leadership growth. Once you understand the central themes of the book, you'll discover your primary leadership dimension through an online assessment or an alternative method in Chapter 2. Most leaders enjoy learning about the characteristics associated with their primary leadership dimensions, and we hope that this process will whet your appetite for deeper insights into your behavior.

While we have a central argument to share with you— that all leaders need to be able to stretch beyond their primary leadership dimensions—the experience will be unique to you. We provide specific steps to help you put this model into action, but your experience will also be shaped by your leadership style, your current role, the culture of your organization, and your personal goals.

Chapter 1

The 8 Dimensions of Leadership

As we pulled together material for this book, we had the pleasure of speaking with leaders in all phases in their careers—from those just getting their feet wet to those who are approaching retirement. Across the board, everyone had learned some important lessons along the way. Many laughed openly about the naïveté that they brought to their first leadership roles, or the fact that they just didn't "get it" at first. Some were so driven that they didn't pay much attention to the needs of the people around them. Others lacked confidence and struggled to make unpopular decisions. One referred to herself as nothing short of a "hard-ass" in her early days as a leader.

Learning to Lead

The fact of the matter is, we all approach leadership from a unique starting point—a combination of our own psychological make-up, intelligence, training, and experience. Life has taught each of us what it means to be a leader, and we probably caught our first glimpses of it as children. As we watched teachers, coaches, parents, and scout leaders, we started to form our own concepts of "leader," and with every new experience, that concept became more complex. Not only did we note examples of outstanding leadership, but we also thought to ourselves, "I'm not going to do that when I'm in charge."

So, well before any of us took on our first leadership roles, we started to imagine what it means to be a leader. And yet, as evidenced by the conversations we had with seasoned leaders, few of us are actually prepared to lead. In many ways, leadership is a learn-by-doing art form, and that's one of the reasons there are so many books out there suggesting the latest and greatest way to lead. And people eat this stuff up, right?

With all of this information out there, why do so many leaders feel ill-prepared? One leader gave us his take on the institutional systems that typically funnel promising people into leadership roles. "When I started at [a large corporation] back in 1981, I was rewarded for being the smartest assistant product manager," he said. Not only was he smart, but he did what management wanted to see. "Beating my peers," he said, "being the first one to answer. Being smarter than them in seeing trends. Pointing things out that other people didn't see. And I got rewarded for that type of get-it-done behavior."

Seems pretty straightforward, right? If you perform your job well and show some hustle, eventually, you'll move up the ranks. "So you do this for a number of years," he added, "and then all of a sudden, someone says, 'Great, we're going to reward you. You're now the head of the operation. And you've got 50 people working for you.'" This is where things got a little more complicated for our leader.

You see, he kept on doing exactly what he'd been doing— exactly what he'd been *rewarded* for. "And guess what?" he asked, "You don't get *rewarded* now—now all of a sudden, people hate you. They're like, 'No—I do it. You need to motivate and inspire me to do it.' And nobody taught me how to do that." Now, our leader had done all of the traditional things that people do to prepare for leadership. He'd been to business school, for example, but still, he was caught off guard by the unique demands placed upon him as a leader. And, in the day-to-day chaos of it all, there was probably little time for conscious reflection on the art of leadership.

What Does Leadership Require?

To be a leader is to make tough decisions—often being forced to choose between competing demands—but what makes it a truly messy endeavor is the fact that people are involved. People, in all of their complex glory, make leadership the art that it is. Leaders often need to orchestrate people around complex goals, deal with people who choose to resist, and try to gain alignment from people with a variety of interests.

As you strive to grow as a leader, you'll need to focus your leadership energy in new directions, and this will sometimes be a stretch for you. While you may land your first leadership role because of your outgoing nature and positive attitude, you may need to develop your analytical side to be more successful in your next role. The more responsibility you gain, the more you will probably be challenged to increase your competencies. Not only will you need to be good with numbers, for example, but you'll need to be seen as someone who can rally the troops when energy is lagging.

The world may not need another book on leadership, but we think you need this book. Why? Because despite all of the courses, books, models, and practical experiences most leaders encounter in their careers, they are often missing something important: *a broad perspective on the range of behaviors that is required to be a truly effective leader.* Our research consistently finds eight dimensions of leadership behavior that organize the large collection of priorities, actions, and attitudes that people demonstrate as they provide effective leadership. While it is currently fashionable to promote a "strengths-based" approach to leadership in which a leader only focuses on competencies that align with natural talents, we find that leaders who try to "outsource" those dimensions that they find less natural ultimately fail.

Multiple Dimensions Matter

It's easy to say, "I don't do the numbers thing." Or, "I leave the inspirational stuff to my sales guys." But the truth is, a one-dimensional leader, no matter how good he or she is at that one thing, can't provide the kind of leadership that leads to innovation, social change, or business transformation. The one-dimensional leader sticks with what he or she knows and avoids using those dimensions that feel less comfortable. This kind of leader lays out a plan to help the team reach its vision, but all too often, reality doesn't cooperate. Without the diverse skills needed to deal with complex challenges, the one-dimensional leader often chooses an inadequate response. Perhaps it's a response with which he or she is comfortable, but it's not appropriate for the situation. The multidimensional leader—say, one who understands the 8 Dimensions of Leadership Model—knows that great leadership requires a wide range of competencies and relationship skills. No person manifests all of these dimensions all of the time; however, every effective leader will need to be able to use each dimension at various points in his or her career.

The 8 Dimensions of Leadership Model is based on the DiSC® model, a systematic way to understand the psychological forces that drive each of us beneath the surface. Our organization has been studying the DiSC model for the past 35 years to understand how people perform and interact in the world of work. Five years ago, we decided to dedicate our resources to understanding how DiSC can help people become better leaders. Through a combination of empirical and theoretical research, we have developed the 8 Dimensions of Leadership. The key leadership dimensions we will be sharing with you in the rest of the book are: Pioneering, Energizing, Affirming, Inclusive, Humble, Deliberate, Resolute, and Commanding.

As you can see in Figure 1.1, "The 8 Dimensions of Leadership Model," the eight dimensions form a circle. This isn't coincidental. Research shows that when the data points describing the meaning of these concepts are compared

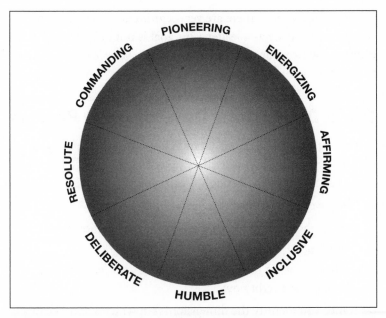

PIONEERING

COMMANDING

ENERGIZING

RESOLUTE

AFFIRMING

DELIBERATE

INCLUSIVE

HUMBLE

Figure 1.1. The 8 Dimensions of Leadership Model

mathematically, they form a circular relationship. In other words, the dimensions are nonhierarchical and nonsequential. A leader has a natural home on the circle, but he or she can move to an adjacent or opposite style depending on the situation or role. Such flexibility is easier for some leaders than for others.

We offer the model as a way to expand your perspective about what constitutes effective leadership. Some of the leadership dimensions described here will seem very familiar to you, while others may seem counterintuitive. Everyone has a psychological comfort zone within the model toward which they gravitate. Think of this particular dimension as your "default setting." Unless we understand the nature of these psychological influences on our work as leaders, we remain captive to our own beliefs, attitudes, and priorities, which can all too often blind us to the reality of a situation and the needs of our organizations. Mastering the 8 Dimensions of Leadership Model will help you reduce how often you jump to conclusions, make poor judgment calls, and project your own motivations onto others. This model will help you see that there are very legitimate alternatives to your default setting as a leader. Our goal is not only to expand your perspective, but also to help you shape your leadership style to match your current situation.

The 8 Dimensions Development Process

We hope that you're excited about the opportunity before you— the chance to expand your leadership framework. We'll help you do this by walking you through a four-step process:

A. Discover your primary leadership dimension

B. Learn about the psychological drivers, motivations, and "blind spots" typical of leaders with your style

C. Reflect on what really matters most in your leadership development right now

D. Once you identify the dimension(s) in which you'd like to grow, learn leadership lessons to help you get there

First, we'll help you discover your default setting on the leadership model. You have two different options to help you identify your primary leadership dimension: We provide a self-assessment method in Chapter 2, or we offer a free online assessment at *www.8DimensionsOfLeadership.com*. If you received an e-mail with a personalized access code from a consultant, you will use this to complete the assessment. Otherwise, you may simply visit the URL printed here.

Once you know your primary leadership dimension, you will find the relevant chapter in Part 2 that will take you on a deep dive into the psychological underpinnings of your style. In order to learn how to shift your leadership style to meet changing demands, you'll need to understand your psychological drivers, motivations, and "blind spots." We are often aware of the benefits that a personality trait provides to us, but less frequently do we recognize the limitations that very same trait might produce. The chapters in Part 2 provide you with a more balanced view of what makes you tick as a leader.

Once you've gained a deeper understanding of the psychology behind both your strengths and challenges, you'll move to Part 3 of the book, which provides some concrete leadership lessons to help you grow as a leader in ways that will be particularly meaningful and beneficial to you personally. In our experience, the lessons that provide the most impact for any individual leader depend not only on his or her primary leadership dimension, but also on his or her current role, the organizational culture, and the leader's personal goals. If you choose not to take the online assessment, the printed Leadership Needs Assessment in Part 3 will help you prioritize which of the eight dimensions to begin working on now.

Each chapter in Part 3 provides a set of three lessons and suggestions to improve your capability as a leader. The lessons were developed to help you see how each dimension contributes to effective leadership. So, if your default dimension is, for example, Commanding, and your responses to the online or printed assessment suggest that you start by learning to be more Inclusive, you'll focus on three lessons based on the talents that Inclusive leaders bring to their organizations. As the demands of your leadership role evolve over time, you can return to the assessment to focus on new lessons.

The Promise of this Process

Change is inevitable. What works for you as a leader today may not work next year. The 8 Dimensions of Leadership will give you a flexible framework that you can take with you through these changes. By understanding your natural home on the model and building your own repertoire of leadership behavior based on what the other seven dimensions offer, you can learn to shift your style to meet the needs of your organization and the people you work with. The model will also provide a strong vocabulary for you to use in solving leadership problems—think of these eight dimensions as a simple language to help you make sense of what it means to be a leader.

Neil—a Resolute leader who is now the president of a manufacturing company—told us that early in his career, he was firmly planted in his own ways and really didn't understand where other people were coming from. "I'm more flexible now," he said, "but back then, it was kind of like, 'How do you lead people like this? They're so weird, they're so different, they're not even like me.'" An added benefit of understanding the eight dimensions is that you may find yourself observing behaviors and trying to place the people you work with in the model.

We found that Neil's overall perspective—that becoming a more effective leader is about expanding one's leadership framework and developing greater flexibility—was consistent among senior-level leaders we interviewed. Looking back on their careers, few leaders suggested that they are completely different people today. Instead, they expressed a sense of being more comfortable "in their own skin." The challenges they faced along the way forced them to stretch their conceptual frameworks of what it means to be a leader, and many of their greatest successes stemmed from moving beyond their respective comfort zones in thought, feeling, and action.

Our hope is that you not only learn to stretch and to grow, but also to feel more comfortable in your own skin as a leader. Your "default" style is valuable, and you can build on it by understanding both its benefits and its limitations. We invite you to approach this book with an open mind and a genuine desire to become a better leader. The goal is to lead like you, only better.

Chapter 2

Discover Your Primary Leadership Dimension

Introduction

Perhaps you're one of the millions of people around the world who have taken a DiSC® assessment through a workplace training session, or, this may be your very first encounter with this simple yet powerful model of human behavior. No matter. Whether you've previously "done DiSC" or not, this book can help you learn the model, discover your own style, and use the 8 Dimensions of Leadership Model to increase your effectiveness as a leader

What, exactly, is DiSC? The DiSC assessment is a tool that helps individuals assess which of several behavioral styles describes them most accurately. By learning their individual DiSC styles, people can gain a better understanding of their own strengths, challenges, fears, and motivators. More importantly, they can learn how to use DiSC to strengthen their relationships with others, building stronger, better-functioning organizations, one relationship at a time.

DiSC 101

Before we dig into the 8 Dimensions of Leadership Model further, we'll provide an overview of the DiSC model. In its simplest form, the DiSC model includes four basic styles—D, i, S, and C. These initials stand for Dominance, Influence, Steadiness, and Conscientiousness. Within each of these four "primary" styles, there is some variation. For example, some people who fall in the D quadrant lean slightly toward the i quadrant, whereas others lean toward C. The former have the Di style—that is, D flavored with i—whereas the latter have the DC style. There is also variation in intensity of the styles. Some people are strongly inclined toward one style, while others are more of a blend of all of the styles. For more information about DiSC, please refer to the Appendix.

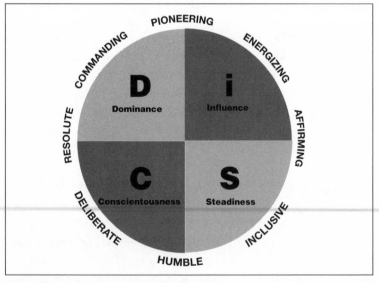

Figure 2.1. The DISC® Model

Origins of the DiSC® Model

In 1928, physiological psychologist Dr. William Moulton Marston (1893–1947) published *Emotions of Normal People*, a book that laid the groundwork for what would become today's DiSC assessments. Marston was interested in theories that helped explain emotions and their physical manifestations. In *Emotions of Normal People*, Marston proposed that people express their emotions through four primary responses.

According to Marston, the four primary types of emotional expression are related to how a person perceives him- or herself in relation to the environment. Marston organized these self-perceptions in a two-axis model. While the original model was quite technical, it can be best understood in terms of favorability and power. The first axis shows whether a person perceives the environment as favorable or unfavorable. The second axis shows a person's perception of his or her own power within the environment. Specifically, this axis measures whether a person views him- or herself as more or less powerful than the environment.

By weighing a person's self-perceptions of these two axes, Marston proposed that his or her emotional state could be described using one of four DiSC behavioral styles. While Marston didn't develop a psychological instrument to measure his theoretical model or determine one's primary DiSC style over time, many researchers have continued to develop and refine such instruments over the past 80 years. While the labels for the four DiSC styles have changed, Marston's original theory remains the archetype of modern DiSC instruments such as the DiSC model described here.

Placing Yourself on the 8 Dimensions of Leadership Model

Now that you understand the basics of DiSC, we'll describe the two main axes of the 8 Dimensions of Leadership Model to give you a sense of the behaviors associated with different areas of the model. If you aren't sure of your DiSC style, this should help you begin to identify which of the eight dimensions resonate most with you.

Two Axes of the Model

First, imagine that there is a north-south axis running down the center of the circular 8 Dimensions of Leadership Model. On one end of this axis—the northern end—are those dimensions that include more fast-paced and outspoken qualities: Commanding, Pioneering, and Energizing. Leaders who tend toward these styles prefer high-energy environments where they can act quickly and try new things. They tend to get bored with repetitive tasks, and they may grow restless when expected to work methodically for long stretches of time. Personal power is important to them, and they long to play a vital role in the organizations in which they're involved. They often have a high need for recognition, and they may grow frustrated in environments where they don't feel their talents are being put to good use. Leaders with these styles tend to be confident, and they're rarely timid about sharing their opinions.

On the other end are those dimensions that include more cautious and reflective qualities: Deliberate, Humble, and Inclusive. Leaders who primarily use these dimensions prefer structured environments where they can work methodically to ensure stability. They tend to be fairly careful, and they often favor tried-and-true methods over radical innovations. Reliability is important to them, and they strive to serve their organizations responsibly and consistently. They don't like to be in the spotlight, and they may grow frustrated in environments where people seem more concerned with getting ahead than doing a good job.

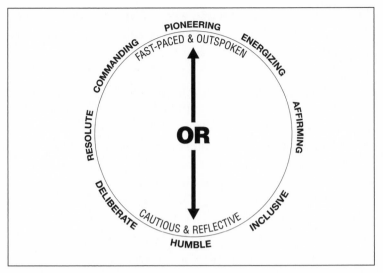

Figure 2.2. The North-South Axis

These leaders are often more reserved, so they tend to use more understated leadership behaviors.

Consider which end of the north-south axis sounds most like you. You may feel like you're firmly planted at one end or the other, or you may be less sure. When it comes to your default behaviors, it's possible to fall anywhere along the axis, from the edge of the circular model to the center.

Next, picture a second axis—a west-east axis running across the middle of the model. On the western side of the axis, you'll find those dimensions that feature more skeptical and questioning tendencies: Deliberate, Resolute, and Commanding. Leaders who primarily use these dimensions naturally ask a lot of questions. In fact, they often approach new ideas—and new people—with skepticism. They like to solve problems, and they may even be energized by the challenge of overcoming an unexpected obstacle. Competency is important to them, and they want to be seen as capable of working independently to deliver on their promises. They often have a high need to be right, and they may become argumentative when others call their logic into question. Leaders who primarily use these dimensions usually try to be objective, and they don't like to let emotions play a part in their decisions.

On the eastern side of this axis, you'll find those dimensions that feature more warm and accepting behaviors: Energizing, Affirming, and Inclusive. Leaders who primarily use these dimensions want to create friendly environments where people and ideas are respected. They want everyone to get along, and they may struggle to handle conflict. Because collaboration is important to them, they strive to make other people feel like important members of their team. They often reach out to others with praise and encouragement, and they may dislike working closely with people who they see as critical. Leaders who primarily use these dimensions are accepting, and they tend to focus on the positive qualities of other people and ideas. Reflect on which end of this axis sounds most like you.

Most likely, you've been able to identify approximately where you fall on each of the two axes. Keep in mind that

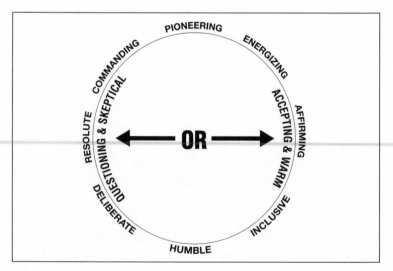

Figure 2.3. The West-East Axis

concepts located across from each other on the circular model are theoretically opposed. Therefore, most people tend to gravitate toward one end of each axis, though some are, indeed, in the middle. While you no doubt exhibit qualities of all eight of the dimensions from time to time, one area of the circular model is likely your emotional stronghold—the set of consistent leadership behaviors that you rely on by default. Take a moment to select the area of the model that sounds most like you. For example, if you suspect that you're most comfortable in the southeastern corner of the model, chances are good that your primary dimension is the Inclusive Dimension, but you'll want to look carefully at Affirming and Humble as well.

Self-Assessment Options

You have three self-assessment options to identify your primary leadership dimesion:

1) Online assessment,

2) Previous DiSC assessment, or

3) Estimation based on written descriptions.

If you received an e-mail with a personalized access code from a consultant, click on the link to take your assessment. If not, you can use the online assessment at *www.8DimensionsOfLeadership.com* to identify your primary leadership dimension more accurately. If you already know your DiSC style from a previous assessment, you can line it up with the corresponding leadership dimension, as shown in Table 2.1. If you don't know your DiSC style and prefer not to use the online assessment, the rest of this chapter provides descriptions to help you to estimate your primary leadership dimension by gaining a better understanding of each dimension. As we travel around the circular model, you'll be able to home in on which of the eight leadership dimensions sounds most like you.

Dimension	DiSC Style(s)
Pioneering	Di, iD
Energizing	i
Affirming	iS, Si
Inclusive	S
Humble	SC, CS
Deliberate	C
Resolute	CD, DC
Commanding	D

Table 2.1. DiSC Styles and the 8 Dimensions of Leadership

The Pioneering Dimension

Leaders who primarily use the Pioneering Dimension tend to be adventurous, dynamic, and charismatic. Their optimistic and persuasive style often inspires others to join their efforts, and because they're good at making connections, they're often able to leverage relationships to help reach their ambitious goals. They tend to be extremely action-oriented, and they may be impulsive at times. Because they want to make exciting breakthroughs, they're naturally drawn to new opportunities, and they may sometimes move ahead without considering how their decisions could affect others.

Pioneering Leaders in Action

At their best: bold, passionate leaders who inspire others to take chances on new directions. At their worst: impulsive, overconfident leaders who use their charm to gain support for wild ideas.

Goals	Quick action, new opportunities, exciting breakthroughs
Judges others by	Confidence, influence, ability to think creatively
Influences others by	Charm, bold action, passion
Overuses	Impatience, egotism, impulsiveness, outspokenness
Under pressure	Becomes aggressive, overpowers others, becomes impulsive
Fears	Loss of power, stifling environments, loss of attention
Would increase effectiveness through	Patience, humility, consideration

Table 2.2. The Pioneering Leader at a Glance

The Energizing Dimension

Leaders who primarily use the Energizing Dimension tend to be spontaneous, outgoing, and encouraging. They're often enthusiastic about new opportunities, and they aren't afraid to take an exciting idea and run with it. Because these leaders have a strong need for variety, they often generate more ideas than they're able to implement. They tend to be more collaborative than other fast-paced leaders, and they may struggle to complete solitary tasks that offer little opportunity for interaction. They're extremely eager to connect with others who can help them realize their big-picture vision. However, in between flurries of activity, they may sometimes drop the ball on specifics and follow-through.

Energizing Leaders in Action

At their best: upbeat, eager leaders who are willing to take chances on colorful new ideas. At their worst: scattered, erratic leaders who see little need for consistency.

Goals	Popularity, approval, excitement
Judges others by	Openness, social skills, enthusiasm
Influences others by	Charm, optimism, energy, personal connection
Overuses	Optimism, praise, enthusiasm
Under pressure	Becomes disorganized, gets overly expressive, becomes frantic
Fears	Rejection, not being heard, not being liked
Would increase effectiveness through	Being more objective, following through on tasks

Table 2.3. The Energizing Leader at a Glance

The Affirming Dimension

Leaders who primarily use the Affirming Dimension tend to be friendly, approachable, and positive. They often make a point of acknowledging other people's contributions, and this may breed loyalty among their colleagues. Because they have a high need for harmony, they work hard to create a positive environment where everyone can work in peace, free of fear or excessive conflict. Compared to other leaders with similar styles, they tend to be more easygoing. They don't have the fast-paced style of the Energizing Dimension, nor do they have the same degree of caution seen in the Inclusive Dimension. Because they want to make others feel comfortable, they tend to have an open-door policy, and they may fail to deliver tough feedback to others.

Affirming Leaders in Action

At their best: kind, supportive leaders who work to create a respectful, positive environment. At their worst: indirect, conflict-averse leaders who fail to hold others accountable.

Goals	Friendship, acceptance, close relationships
Judges others by	Ability to see good in others, warmth, approachability
Influences others by	Agreeableness, empathy, being patient
Overuses	Patience with others, indirect approaches, personal connections
Under pressure	Takes criticism personally, tries to make everyone happy
Fears	Pressuring others, being disliked, facing aggression
Would increase effectiveness through	Acknowledging others' flaws, confronting problems

Table 2.4. The Affirming Leader at a Glance

The Inclusive Dimension

Leaders who primarily use the Inclusive Dimension tend to be diplomatic, accepting, and patient. They're most comfortable in a stable environment where they can work steadily toward their goals, so they're often wary of ideas that would require rapid change. Because these leaders want to be seen as dependable, they often prefer to work at a methodical pace to ensure that they have time to address specifics. They tend to be optimistic, and this can sometimes cause them to overestimate other people's abilities. They're careful to include others in meaningful dialogue before moving ahead with major decisions, and because they often go out of their way to accommodate everyone, they may struggle to make timely decisions.

Inclusive Leaders in Action

At their best: sincere, accommodating leaders who collaborate with others to make decisions where everyone wins. At their worst: passive, overly trusting leaders who let others take advantage of their supportive, patient nature.

Goals	Harmony, stability, acceptance
Judges others by	Dependability, sincerity
Influences others by	Accommodating others, consistent performance
Overuses	Modesty, passive resistance, compromise
Under pressure	Gives in, avoids revealing true opinions
Fears	Letting people down, rapid change
Would increase effectiveness through	Displaying self-confidence, revealing true feelings

Table 2.5. The Inclusive Leader at a Glance

The Humble Dimension

Leaders who primarily use the Humble Dimension tend to be soft-spoken, modest, and precise. Their methodical and consistent style often models follow-through and diligence for others. Because they're fair-minded and practical, they're often able to discern what systems and structures would meet other people's needs. They tend to be so cautious that they may hinder spontaneity or creativity at times. Because they want to maintain a stable environment, they're naturally wary of change, and they may favor standard operating procedures over new, innovative methods.

Humble Leaders in Action

At their best: modest, fair-minded leaders who provide reliable outcomes through steadiness and consistency. At their worst: rigid, overly cautious leaders who are afraid to move beyond the status quo.

Goals	Stability, reliable outcomes, calm environment
Judges others by	Precise standards, reliability, even temperament
Influences others by	Practicality, diplomacy, self-control, consistency
Overuses	Traditional methods, sense of caution, humility
Under pressure	Withdraws, gets bogged down, becomes inflexible, gives in
Fears	Emotionally charged situations, ambiguity, time pressure, chaos
Would increase effectiveness through	Being decisive, showing urgency, initiating change, speaking up

Table 2.6. The Humble Leader at a Glance

The Deliberate Dimension

Leaders who primarily use the Deliberate Dimension tend to be systematic, cautious, and analytical. Because ensuring accuracy is vitally important to them, they tend to work at a more moderate pace. They want to be seen as experts, so they're often drawn to projects and roles where they can shape processes to meet their high standards. They tend to be detached and unemotional, and they prefer to work independently. They're highly motivated to get things right the first time, and they may become defensive if people challenge their methods or ideas.

Deliberate Leaders in Action

At their best: conscientious, disciplined leaders who provide high-quality outcomes through careful analysis and planning.
At their worst: risk-averse, perfectionistic leaders who pay little attention to the human element.

Goals	Accuracy, objective processes
Judges others by	Expertise, systematic processes
Influences others by	Logic, exacting standards
Overuses	Analysis, restraint
Under pressure	Overwhelms others with logic, becomes rigid
Fears	Being wrong, strong displays of emotion
Would increase effectiveness through	Acknowledging others' feelings, looking beyond data

Table 2.7. The Deliberate Leader at a Glance

The Resolute Dimension

Leaders who primarily use the Resolute Dimension tend to be challenging, determined, and rational. They set high standards for themselves and others, and they may have little patience for people or practices that seem inefficient. They tend to be blunt, and they aren't afraid to speak up when they see problems with plans or methods, even if it means stepping on some toes. Not only do they want to get efficient results, but they want those results to be of the utmost quality. These leaders want to be seen as highly competent, and they may lose their patience with people or situations that stand in their way.

Resolute Leaders in Action
At their best: questioning, independent leaders who aren't afraid to challenge the status quo to get better results. At their worst: cynical, insensitive leaders who seem intent on putting a negative spin on everything.

Goals	Independence, personal accomplishment, efficient results
Judges others by	Competence, common sense, use of logic
Influences others by	High standards, determination, strict standards
Overuses	Sarcastic or condescending attitude, criticism
Under pressure	Becomes overly critical, ignores people's feelings
Fears	Failure to achieve their standards, lack of control
Would increase effectiveness through	Warmth, tactful communication, paying attention to others' needs

Table 2.8. The Resolute Leader at a Glance

The Commanding Dimension

Leaders who primarily use the Commanding Dimension tend to be competitive, driven, and assertive. They have such a natural take-charge presence that others often look to them for leadership. And, because they want to reach their goals as quickly as possible, they tend to create a sense of urgency for themselves and others. They're often challenging and demanding, and they may be less concerned with social niceties. They're extremely motivated to get results, and in their hurry to reach their goals, they may sometimes show little regard for other people's needs and feelings.

Commanding Leaders in Action
At their best: powerful, decisive leaders who enlist others to work quickly toward ambitious goals. At their worst: forceful, egotistical leaders who push others at the expense of morale.

Goals	Bottom-line results, victory
Judges others by	Ability to achieve results
Influences others by	Assertiveness, insistence, competition
Overuses	Forcefulness, bluntness
Under pressure	Becomes impatient and demanding
Fears	Being taken advantage of, appearing weak
Would increase effectiveness through	Patience, empathy

Table 2.9. The Commanding Leader at a Glance

Summary

After reading this chapter, you should be able to estimate your primary leadership dimension. First, you placed yourself on the two axes—north-south and west-east—to get yourself into the right ballpark. Next, you read descriptions about each dimension. Hopefully, one of these dimensions really resonated with you. If you like, use the figure below to mark your primary leadership dimension. You may wish to validate your self-assessment by asking for input from someone who works closely with you.

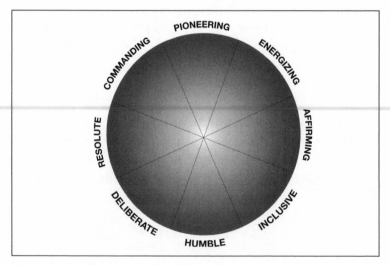

Figure 2.4. My Primary Leadership Dimension

Now that you've decided which of the eight dimensions best describes you, you'll get a chance to learn more about what makes leaders like you tick. In Part 2, the chapter about your primary dimension will describe some of the psychological drivers behind your behavior and help you gain some perspective on your leadership blind spots. You'll walk away from Part 2 with a better sense of your personal leadership style, and this will help you as you reflect on how to best improve your leadership effectiveness in Part 3.

Part 2

A Deeper Dive Into Your Primary Dimension

In Part 1, we provided some background information on DiSC®, described the 8 Dimensions of Leadership, and explained the value of this multidimensional model. Once you gained some baseline knowledge, you had the chance to take the online assessment or place yourself on the model using the information in Chapter 2. Now that you know your primary leadership dimension, it's time to explore one simple but important question: "So what?"

As we've discussed, most leaders use different dimensions as situations call for them, but we all have one default dimension that feels most comfortable. Rest assured that within each style of leadership there is still plenty of room for individuality. However, there are also distinct patterns that we see among leaders with a particular style. By understanding the behaviors that are associated with your primary leadership dimension, you can get a head start on the difficult task of identifying your leadership blind spots—those tendencies that can hold you back from more effective leadership.

In Part 2, we're going to talk about specific psychological drivers that affect how you approach leadership. More specifically, we're going to talk about how these drivers—many of which make you successful in certain areas—can limit your ability to lead effectively. Now, we realize that this isn't generally how people make friends: "Nice to meet you. Let me tell you what you're doing wrong." Before you can really work on improving your effectiveness as a leader, you need to be fully aware of the natural tendencies that you bring to leadership. These tendencies are not only your strengths, but when overused, they can cause you to fall short in other areas. In other words, when you focus too much on your primary leadership dimension, you can unknowingly overlook other dimensions that may be vital in your current situation.

Part of the beauty of the 8 Dimensions of Leadership Model is that it is often able to predict the issues that will pop up for leaders with a particular style. Affirming leaders, for example, tend to have a common set of challenges, some of which stem from a need to feel accepted. Resolute leaders, on the other hand, have another set, some of which are related to a need for personal mastery. The insights that we present in this section are built not only on decades of DiSC research, but also on a wealth of knowledge from the broader field of psychology. Our goal was to take that information and put it into a form that's accessible to real-world leaders.

Not every issue that we bring up in your chapter is going to resonate with you. Some of the psychological drivers that we discuss may be problems that you dealt with a long time ago. Other areas may never have been a problem for you personally. Our hope, however, is to get the wheels turning—to help you dig deeper into some of the hidden assumptions and needs that drive you to lead the way you do. So, we encourage you to turn to the chapter about your primary leadership dimension. Your job is simply to read your chapter and honestly ask yourself, "Do I do that?"

Chapter 3

The Pioneering Leader

Pioneering leaders cut through the brush and inspire the group to venture into uncharted territory. They have a natural passion to grow, expand, and explore. These leaders seize on opportunities that others might not even recognize. We'll elaborate on the value of the Pioneering leader in Chapter 11, but in this chapter, we want to look under the hood to understand what makes this style of leader tick. More specifically, we want to help Pioneering leaders understand some of the hidden psychological mechanisms that can hold them back.

If you're a Pioneering leader, you're probably fairly high-energy and outspoken. People might regard you as charming and confident, and you're more likely to take chances than others. Erin, the vice president of a national political organization, told us, "I think the best description I've ever heard of my personality was [when] somebody said that I was Type A masquerading as smooth jazz." Hiding beneath your exterior are deeper motivations, needs, and assumptions that drive you to act the way you do. The more you understand these drivers, the more you'll be able to consciously control and shape your leadership style.

Based on our research and experience talking to Pioneering leaders, the qualities listed below have a significant impact on how you lead.

- An attraction to adventure
- Consciousness of status
- A bias toward action
- Confidence in your own vision
- A desire to be important
- Enjoyment in the act of persuading and charming others

Reviewing this list, you may recognize that many of these qualities lead to your greatest strengths as a leader. As we discuss these qualities, however, we'll put more emphasis on how they might limit your effectiveness. While you might not identify with all of these qualities, our experience has shown that a number of them probably describe you better than you may initially think.

An Attraction to Adventure

Pioneering leaders are driven to keep seeking bigger and better, and the act of exploration is central to their enjoyment of life. They assume that the goal is to take in more and more. They tend to have very high energy levels, and along with this comes a high need for excitement. Because of this, they tend to be risk-takers, and they don't mind being under pressure. In fact, they're more likely to view pressure as a positive thing.

Leaders with your approach don't like feeling constrained. In fact, they have a high need for freedom. They tend to see a big, wide world of opportunity. People with other styles tend to put artificial psychological constraints on what they can or can't do, but this isn't true for Pioneering leaders. In fact, they're more likely to stretch the boundaries and sidestep the rules. Their combination of desire to explore and high self-confidence leads them to believe that the rules don't really apply to them. Pioneering leaders often have a sense that they see things that other people don't; this helps them take chances, because they assume that things are bound to work out. Since they don't always play by the rules, Pioneering leaders can often buck conformity to jump-start a dying organization or propel it toward new heights.

While you're probably great at leading the group into new territory, that's just one side of the coin. The other side is addressing the internal needs of the group. While you spend a good deal of energy convincing others to get on board with your ever-expanding vision, you may not take the time to understand the needs of your people. Because you're busy driving toward your goals, others may feel that you're simply inviting them to accompany you on your quest. The danger of this egocentric point of view is that by expecting people to adapt to you and your vision, you may lose touch with the evolving needs of the group.

Consciousness of Status

Pioneering leaders are generally interested in moving up the ranks. They seek more important positions, and they tend to be conscious of status; they may be more accommodating of the needs of people who they see as important players. However, their default behavior may be to overlook other people's needs. This isn't an intentional thing—they're simply so engrossed in their own passions that they spend much of their energy convincing others how fantastic their ideas are. At times, they can err on the side of one-way communication. They love to talk, and verbal self-expression provides great emotional rewards for Pioneering leaders. This concept may be totally foreign to people who are less inclined to use the Pioneering Dimension.

While Pioneering leaders can often look upwards and meet the needs of supposedly important people, they sometimes have less interest in catering to the needs of those below them. In fact, they may not know how to figure out what those needs are. At best, Pioneering leaders will sometimes assimilate some group needs into their own vision; that is, they will squeeze those needs into their existing structure. However, they are less likely to actually *accommodate*—or overhaul—their visions to meet a group's needs. Accommodating the group's needs would require you to step outside of your own engaging internal world, and this may mean compromising your own vision. You're probably used to getting other people to adapt to your vision, not the other way around.

A Bias toward Action

Pioneering leaders have a natural ability to be spontaneous that stems from their belief that they are well-equipped to adapt to emerging situations. They tend to be quick thinkers and quick talkers, and others may have trouble keeping up with them. They have a constant need for stimulation and variety, and this can make processes and structure less interesting to them. In fact, they may sometimes find themselves more interested in starting a project than in following through. When it comes to the routine parts, they may grow restless, and they may not take a lot of satisfaction in steady progress. They're more attracted to the big score—progressing in leaps and bounds. Much of the time, they're happy to delegate the details.

What's at the heart of your spontaneity? Generally speaking, your mental outlook is probably more focused on the rewards of success than on the consequences of failure. This perspective allows you not only to act spontaneously, but also to take risks and promote bold action. Whereas people on the southern side of the model might be at a loss to improvise, leaders with your style see it as an opportunity. Sure, it's a cliché, but it's true—you tend to look at problems as opportunities.

Leaders like you aren't afraid to take shortcuts as you come up with quick solutions, and this can be a great asset as a leader because it allows the group to move quickly. However, the same expediency can also cause you to overlook systemic problems. For example, you can get so immersed in the 80/20 mindset that you grow accustomed to operations not being entirely well-oiled. This can be healthy to an extent, but it also allows you to gradually accept work processes that are far less than ideal. When you're so focused on pushing forward, it's easy to let the inner workings of the organization get a little rusty, and, because you have such a strong bias toward action, you may not always spend a lot of time observing, listening, and asking questions.

Confidence in Your Own Vision

Pioneering leaders often have so much confidence in their own vision that they don't see the need to build more structure around it. They tend to see things very clearly in their heads, regardless of how clear it would be if they explained their plans to others. They have a tendency to gloss over the specifics, and they may have a false sense of how well things are actually planned out. This lack of awareness sometimes gets them off the hook from having to go in and work out specific processes. Because things seem so straightforward, they don't feel a nagging sense that more structure and processes are needed before moving ahead. Plans often feel ironed out to Pioneering leaders, even when others would describe them as quite loose.

Leaders like you trust their instincts, and they often keep track of things in their heads. They may feel that they know their work "by heart"—that they have a good big-picture handle on all of the mechanisms for which they're responsible. Pioneering leaders have gut feelings about how things should proceed, and they'll often step in to correct processes when they see something that strays from their vision. They may do this on the fly, sometimes addressing problems before taking the time to explore the complexity. This often results in a solution that addresses most of the problem but may leave smaller residual issues that will come up later.

Further, because they're good at persuading and charming others, Pioneering leaders often come to believe their own press. The more they project their opinions with absolute confidence, the more internal confidence they have in those ideas. This is where they get into trouble. Take, for example, a study that followed the predictions made by political pundits for twenty years (Tetlock, 2005). First of all, they found that the pundits were no more accurate than the average well-informed person. But more interestingly, they found that the more frequently the experts were cited in the press and the more well-known the experts were, the more likely they were to be wrong. The more confident they were, the less accurate they were. The takeaway? Just because you can convince other people to see things your way doesn't make your way right. A good salesperson can sell just about anything, but this doesn't make your judgment infallible.

A Desire to Be Important

Pioneering leaders often describe themselves as being people-oriented—and in many respects, they are—but they also do have higher ego needs than leaders with, say, Humble as their primary dimension. Pioneering leaders often come across as extremely confident and charismatic. However, they have a fundamental, usually subconscious, insecurity that they are not as important as they desire to be. To deal with this insecurity, they often protect themselves by creating an exaggerated concept of self-importance. Much like Commanding leaders, they cope with their insecurities by focusing on their idealized selves and pushing aside their fears. While they're usually happy to bring others along for the ride, they do have an internal mechanism that pushes them to seek higher personal status.

The fact that others will follow them feeds their feelings of pride and self-worth. For the same reason, Pioneering leaders often want to be associated with the "in" crowd. They're particularly interested in being around "larger than life" people who show the most promise for creating exciting opportunities. People with your Pioneering approach don't want to be stuck in the undifferentiated middle. They feel that they belong at the top, and they tend to believe that, given a fair chance, they will be given increasingly powerful positions. The idea of being powerless is extremely agitating, and they tend to believe that they have the power to shape their environment. If their power or influence is stripped away, it shakes them deeply.

Enjoyment in the Act of Persuading and Charming Others

Pioneering leaders often use their charm to open doors. People are attracted to leaders who are dynamic, energetic, and perhaps even funny. Pioneering leaders have a way of connecting with people—of inviting them into their exciting world—even if only on a superficial level. They not only have a strong vision of how things should be, but they have the confidence and the verbal skills to describe it. The act of persuading people can be very gratifying for Pioneering leaders, both in one-on-one and in team settings. Not only is it about forging connections, but it's about the challenge of getting people to see things in a new way. When Pioneering leaders are successful in using their charisma to sway others, it reinforces their feelings of importance and power: "If I can persuade people, I am important. If I am important, I am good."

Not only are Pioneering leaders good sellers, but they're also good closers. They have the ambition to get things rolling, and they'll push hard to get things finalized. While leaders with your style are able to cultivate relationships, they also don't mind applying pressure when they need to. In fact, you may be willing to risk damaging a relationship to get what you want. Not only that, but you have a knack for instinctively recognizing what other people want and using that to your advantage. For example, when trying to motivate someone, you may hint at the possibility of recognition or a promotion. At times, you may even resort to intimidating tactics as you pour on the pressure. Yet, because you have such a charming way about you, you're often able to return the relationship to a collegial state once compliance is assured. It may be unconscious, but most Pioneering leaders know how to use their power, and few people can resist the desire to be in the good graces of someone so interpersonally powerful.

Leaders are responsible for rallying and empowering people. Pioneering leaders do one side of this extremely well. They share their passion by painting a colorful picture of their vision, and they're often able to get people excited, but after the inspirational speeches, they're not always there to offer people support. They're often too focused on advancing their ideas and driving toward their goals. All too often, people start to feel that the Pioneering leaders they work with aren't really interested in supporting them or listening to them. If Pioneering leaders aren't more intentional about this, they can lose followers along the way.

How to Navigate the Rest of the Book

You've had a chance to read about some of the psychological drivers that may hold you back as a leader, but what about the good stuff? What about the areas where you naturally excel? Chapter 11 in Part 3 is designed to highlight exactly that: the assets that Pioneering leaders bring to the table. There you'll find the three lessons that everyone else can learn from leaders like you.

But, of course, other leaders have things to teach you as well. Looking at the model, you may have noticed that the Pioneering Dimension is opposite the Humble Dimension. Chances are that you may need to focus on this dimension, but depending on your individual situation, there may be others that are more important. Next, go to Part 3, where you'll explore the lessons that are most important for you right now.

Chapter 4

The Energizing Leader

O f all of the leaders we will discuss in this book, Energizing leaders have the easiest time generating enthusiasm for an idea. They have a contagious sense of optimism that engages people, and they help the group build an invaluable network of connections. We'll elaborate on the value of the Energizing leader in Chapter 12, but in this chapter we want to dig a little deeper to understand what is going on behind all of that energy. More specifically, we want to help Energizing leaders understand some of the unobservable psychological mechanisms that can hold them back.

If you're an Energizing leader, you're probably outgoing and sociable. People readily pick up on your enthusiasm, and you're rarely at a loss for words. Beneath this extremely positive exterior are deeper motivations, needs, and assumptions that drive you to act the way you do. The more you understand these drivers, the more you'll be able to consciously control and shape your leadership style.

Based on our research and experience talking to Energizing leaders, the qualities listed below have a significant impact on how you lead.

- A spirited drive
- A preference for the experiential over the analytical
- A desire to avoid tension
- A drive for forward momentum
- A desire to express your enthusiasm
- A tendency to speak freely and fluidly

Most likely, these qualities are the source of some of your greatest strengths as a leader. As we review the list above, however, we'll be paying a little more attention to how they might hinder your leadership performance. While you might not identify with all of these qualities, our experience has shown that a number of them probably describe you better than you may initially think.

A Spirited Drive

Energizing leaders often describe themselves as high-spirited and full of life. Like other leaders whose styles fall on the northern side of the model, Energizing leaders are fast-paced and on the go. Because they're always on the lookout for fun and adventure, leaders like you are often open to big changes that more cautious folks might see as reckless. You may not necessarily see yourself as a big risk-taker, but most leaders with your style are willing to jump into exciting opportunities without many reservations.

When you're excited to implement a new idea, slowing down to address details and potential obstacles probably holds little appeal. You're more likely to dig right in and get started, and you're probably comfortable improvising as problems arise. As long as you have a plan that you feel good about, you may believe that hard work and a positive attitude will take you where you need to go. Because you're so enthusiastic, you tend to focus on the positive when envisioning the outcomes of a new initiative. In fact, you may wonder why anyone would *want* to focus on the potential negative outcomes.

Because leaders with your style are so optimistic, they have faith that things will always work out for the best. In fact, leaders like you may even have a selective memory that focuses more on successes than on failures. Energizing leaders often feel that their gut instincts are especially sharp, when, in truth, they may not always be in tune with reality. They tend to take action because it feels right, and they don't necessarily address potential problems and contingency plans. When they're drawn to a colorful idea, they just want to act on it immediately.

A Preference for the Experiential Over the Analytical

Energizing leaders often prefer to gain information experientially rather than through analysis. Leaders with other styles may need to sort out all of the details and understand how the pieces fit together before they're comfortable saying that an idea has come together. However, leaders with your approach tend to have a lower threshold for reaching this type of certainty. You may focus on the major points, assuming that you'll be able to deal with the details later, and if you detect potentially messy problems that might not support your plan, you tend to gloss over them. By filtering information in this way, you're able to protect your vision and keep it perfect in your mind.

Gathering information through analysis is really the opposite of trusting your gut. It involves stepping back from the situation to observe and to think, and this may seem way less exciting to you than jumping into an experience and relying on your intuition to sense what does and doesn't seem to work. Energizing leaders require a good deal of stimulation, and they may see difficult, potentially frustrating analyses as boring or even painful. At times, they may start things that they don't finish, often because they get distracted or become bored. Sitting down to analyze a plan may not seem immediately rewarding to you, so you may move on to a more colorful task or a social endeavor. However, by skimping on analysis, you may come across as flighty or disorganized to people who are more analytical. People whose styles fall in on the western side of the model are more questioning and skeptical, and they want to see that their leaders have examined plans carefully.

Energizing leaders are sometimes described as being unstructured and less detail oriented, and this is sometimes the case. However, they can also be quite organized. In general, leaders with your style are attracted to strong positive emotions, like fun and excitement, so they're less likely to get wrapped up in *mundane* details or to do things systematically. These things require discipline, which doesn't lead to immediate gratification. When getting organized *feels* good—and it does to many people—the Energizing leader is all about it. But when attending to the details feels tedious or ceases to be gratifying, Energizing leaders lose interest. Rather than push through the frustration of analyzing problems and asking tough questions, you may often choose the path of least resistance.

A Desire to Avoid Tension

Energizing leaders want to keep things pleasant, so they have a very low tolerance for negative emotions and experiences. In fact, they try to put unpleasant things out of their minds as much as possible. While they seem confident on the surface, they're often quite sensitive to criticism, and they tend to take things personally. Energizing leaders are also highly expressive, and when things get heated, they've been known to have emotional outbursts. When too many negative emotions get piled up, they can become overwhelmed and lash out at others. Of course, this leads to more tension, which they like to avoid, so their emotional nature can make for a lot of ups and downs.

As you can see, leaders like you have a lot at stake when it comes to conflict, so it's natural that you tend to avoid it. The process of calling out problems means initiating tension, or at the very least, facing it head-on by telling people to do things differently. To really tackle problems as a leader, you need to make decisions that aren't always popular, stand firm against resistance, and be willing to tolerate it when people grumble about you behind your back. Approval is so important to you that when it's taken away—in the form of rejection, being insulted, or being excluded—you're likely to take it harder than most. Leaders like you are hard-wired to crave popularity and acceptance, so it's natural that you may shy away from confronting problems. Working out sticky issues is probably *not* what you find rewarding about leadership. Energizing leaders are more likely to enjoy the excitement, the attention, the chance to interact with and direct people, and the feeling of making a difference.

A Drive for Forward Momentum

As we've discussed, leaders whose approaches fall on the northern side of the model tend to be fast-paced and outspoken, so Energizing leaders are most attracted to high-energy environments. Variety is important to leaders like you, and you may find that your motivation really lags when things feel stagnant. In general, you'd probably rather start working on whatever's next than try to refine current processes. Because you want to maintain forward momentum, you may find tackling messy problems to be really frustrating. Even if you're successful in solving the problems, it may feel like a waste of time, since you haven't done anything new.

We're not suggesting that leaders like you ignore problems entirely. You probably do your best to respond to crises, but what you may avoid is dealing with process inefficiencies, interpersonal conflicts, and communication gaps. As long as there are new opportunities on the horizon—and you constantly look for them—you'll be inclined to leave well enough alone. You're far more interested in imagining the future than dwelling on the past or getting caught up in today's problems.

A Desire to Express Your Enthusiasm

Energizing leaders have a high need to express their emotions, and this can affect their ability to communicate clearly. Not everyone is so expressive—in fact, many leaders actually *fear* showing emotion or sentimentality. You probably find it emotionally rewarding to express yourself, and it may not occur to you to be self-conscious. You have less of a verbal filter than people who are more cautious and reflective. This isn't necessarily a bad thing—your open communication style, spontaneity, and passion are what make you such an engaging storyteller. However, you may embellish facts at times to make your experiences seem more dramatic and exciting, and you may not always communicate so effectively when trying to convey less exciting, albeit important, information.

As we've discussed, Energizing leaders focus on the positive. You have a lot of enthusiasm to share, and you're drawn to others who have fun stories to tell. However, because you're so passionate, you may sometimes monopolize conversations. This is probably a largely unconscious act; you may simply keep relating the conversation back to you. At other times, however, you probably show a keen interest in what's going on in someone else's life, wanting to know all of the details. Overall, your enthusiasm probably helps you connect with many people, but it can also cost you credibility with others. Those who are more questioning and skeptical often shut down when they sense too many exclamation points coming out of your mouth.

A Tendency to Speak Freely and Fluidly

When Energizing leaders converse with others, they are highly engaged. Every interaction is the chance to start or build a relationship. Conversation is very experiential for leaders like you, and you're rarely bound by any self-conscious, analytical forces. People who are more reserved often hold in an idea, wondering whether it's valid or if there's evidence to back it up. You, on the other hand, tend to be comfortable speaking your mind, often as a relaxed stream of consciousness. In doing so, you may not always take the time to consider what the listener needs to hear in order to understand the message. As a result, some of your ideas may be only loosely connected.

There are advantages to being so open about sharing your thoughts and opinions. However, because you offer so many ideas, some of which are clearly *not* your best, some people may start to take what you say with a grain of salt, and people who do take your words seriously may become confused or frustrated since your range of suggestions can lead to false starts. For example, you may think that you're just throwing out a bunch of ideas, while someone might take the first one you suggest and run with it, only to find out that you've moved on to something else. If people don't understand your steam of consciousness approach, they may question your judgment, especially if they're more analytical. Leaders like you don't intend to be "big talkers" or scattered—in fact, you may see yourself as quite organized— but you can get so excited about new ideas that you may have trouble sticking to one clear message. Your message may feel disjointed, with updates relayed in a piecemeal fashion, and people may not grasp what your actual plan is.

How to Navigate the Rest of the Book

You've had a chance to read about some of the psychological drivers that may hold you back as a leader, but what about the good stuff? What about the areas where you naturally excel? Chapter 12 in Part 3 is designed to highlight exactly that: the assets that Energizing leaders bring to the table. There you'll find the three lessons that everyone else can learn from leaders like you.

But, of course, other leaders have things to teach you as well. Looking at the model, you may have noticed that the Energizing Dimension is opposite the Deliberate Dimension. Chances are that you may need to focus on this dimension, but depending on your individual situation, there may be others that are more important. Next, go to Part 3, where you'll explore the lessons that are most important for you right now.

Chapter 5

The Affirming Leader

As you might expect, Affirming leaders have a pretty positive vibe about them. They excel at building morale and creating a supportive environment. They're quick to acknowledge the contributions of their team members and to show people just how much their efforts and talents are appreciated. We'll elaborate on the value of the Affirming leader in Chapter 13, but in this chapter, we want to go behind the scenes to understand what makes these leaders tick. More specifically, we want to help Affirming leaders understand some of the more subtle psychological mechanisms that can hold them back.

If you're an Affirming leader, you probably have an easy, cheerful demeanor. People instantly pick up on your warmth and sincerity, and they probably find you extremely easy to talk to. Clearly, there are deeper motivations, needs, and assumptions underneath this friendly exterior that drive you to act the way you do. The more you understand these drivers, the more you'll be able to consciously control and shape your leadership style.

Based on our research and experience talking to Affirming leaders, the qualities listed below may have a significant impact on how you lead.

- A relationship orientation
- An open posture
- A need for acceptance and affection
- An aversion to conflict
- A tendency to put problems out of mind
- An avoidance of complex analysis

In a very real sense, these qualities may contribute to some of your most admirable strengths as a leader. As we review these qualities, however, we'll be paying a little more attention to how they might hold you back. While you might not identify with all of these qualities, our experience has shown that a number of them probably describe you better than you may initially think.

A Relationship Orientation

Affirming leaders are typically more relationship-oriented than results-oriented. To them, leadership is more about people than meeting deadlines or making profits. Sure, you have goals, but you may not always have a sense of urgency. Your worldview can create a healthy climate that enables people to balance their personal and professional obligations, but on the flip side, it also makes it easy for people to get too comfortable. Chances are, you don't want to be seen as a taskmaster, and the idea of burdening others is probably unappealing to you. Of all of the leadership styles, Affirming leaders are most likely to describe themselves as empathic. Drive and balance don't have to be mutually exclusive, but they often are if not managed carefully.

Because relationships are so important to Affirming leaders, they often embrace a "do-no-harm" philosophy. They don't want to be the source of anyone's pain. So, rather than call people out on problems or mistakes, they tend to be forgiving. In fact, you may not even recognize people's flaws when you should. Because you feel a duty to keep other people happy, you tend to give them the benefit of the doubt. At times, you may be naïve about a person's true motivation, because it's tough to get your head around the idea that someone could be manipulative or dishonest with you. Even when you do see so-called flaws in another person, you're likely to look past them to see the goodness inside.

An Open Posture

Affirming leaders have an open posture toward life, which means they're not only flexible, but also infinitely patient and tolerant. They can learn to live with delays and obstacles without getting frustrated or showing irritation. Some Affirming leaders may need more structure than others, but in general, they're more interested in going with the flow. They take problems as they come, and they do their best to meet other people's needs while looking for a solution.

Your openness and flexibility may hinder your ability to draw a line in the sand and take control. In general, taking a firm stance and saying something along the lines of "this is what we're going to do—no excuses" is not your style. You're more likely to take individual needs into account and to recognize special circumstances. As a result, setting and sticking to firm deadlines and policies can be difficult for leaders like you because it seems arbitrary and unfair not to be responsive to the needs of the people around you. This type of flexibility is fine on occasion, but there's also a danger that the rules become meaningless. Being too responsive can send the message that goals and results are always negotiable.

A Need for Acceptance and Affection

Affirming leaders find huge value in the social realm of life, and being accepted by others is a big part of this. Early on, leaders with your approach tend to develop an assumption that if they can fit in, belong to the community, and connect with others, then they are valuable as people. On a subconscious level, your mission in life is to belong and be accepted. Because you have this perspective, you've probably developed many genuine traits such as being caring, warm, cooperative, trusting, cheerful, receptive, and agreeable. After all, if getting along with others is the goal, these are important tools to have in your box.

If you need to feel accepted to be content, receiving affection is even better. True affection is not just praise—though you probably don't mind that either—but it's mutual goodwill that people feel toward each other. It's a feeling of connection and of not being alone. It's easy to think of this ideal in romantic relationships, but it also exists in platonic friendships and familial relationships, and Affirming leaders are often able to achieve this level of intimacy without it feeling awkward. How does that impact your leadership performance? On the positive side, you're likely to form friendly relationships with many of the people who you lead. On the challenging side, it can be more difficult for leaders like you to hold people accountable.

An Aversion to Conflict

Leaders with your Affirming approach often struggle to challenge other people's ideas or to give tough feedback. In situations where there is indecision or disagreement, you may often take an indirect path. Because you tend to be so diplomatic and accommodating, it's probably rare for you to be in the middle of a conflict. However, when you're indirectly involved in a disagreement, you may unconsciously—irrationally—take responsibility. Other times, Affirming leaders like you may take on the role of highly diplomatic peacemaker, although you may lack the assertiveness to really command the attention of people who are steeped in anger.

While more forceful leaders often bulldoze their way through a mess that others have created, Affirming leaders tend to explore the situation carefully as they seek consensus. They respect the structures and conventions that others have made, and they seek to get things done in a harmonious way. They often don't fight for their ideas, and as a consequence, they may have trouble "closing the deal." Pushing people in such an aggressive way to get a solid, definite commitment may simply feel too forceful to you. After all, force is the opposite of cooperation, so it's natural that giving the hard sell would be uncomfortable for you. So, while you probably feel comfortable sharing your ideas freely, you may be less likely to push others to see things your way when you encounter resistance.

A Tendency to Put Problems out of Mind

If a problem doesn't have an obvious, easy fix, many Affirming leaders prefer to put it out of their minds. Our research shows that the leadership behavior most commonly requested of Affirming leaders is to increase efficiency by improving methods. Unfortunately, leaders like you have such an instinct to see the best in a situation that they often don't see inefficiencies. Further, they don't want to invite the tension that often comes with stopping the presses and making a big production about changing things. So, it's often easier to pop on a pair of rose-colored glasses and take the unpleasantness out of the picture. This is an overarching trend with Affirming leaders—they're good at tuning in the positive and tuning out the negative.

Because you tend to tune out the negative, you may shy away from demanding challenges. If you're like most Affirming leaders, your desire for harmony is so strong that you'll try to escape a difficult situation as quickly as possible. At times, this means abandoning a challenge such as learning a new skill or developing a base of knowledge for a less tense, more fun pursuit. The tension that often accompanies challenging learning opportunities can feel overwhelming. This is not to say that you don't ever push yourself, but because you have a natural tendency to seek the path of least resistance, you may need to be more intentional about it.

An Avoidance of Complex Analysis

Simply put, in-depth analysis may not be your favorite activity. It often involves extended periods of thankless work trying to understand things that don't seem to *want* to be understood.

Even if you like detail—or consider yourself to be detail-oriented—disciplined analysis is much more involved. Inherent in analysis is pushing through ambiguity until you finally see the light at the end of the tunnel. The act of finally understanding something is highly gratifying, and this is the joy that many find in problem solving. But baked into this whole process is the pain of not knowing, not understanding, and feeling lost.

Leaders with your Affirming approach may look for shortcuts, try to gain a "good enough" understanding of the problem, or look to others to do the disciplined analysis. Why is this often the case for leaders with your style? Again, it's because leaders like you are hardwired to be attracted to positive emotion. Rather than steep yourself in the dark intensity of problem solving, your instinct is to find the crack of light in the cave and escape into the sunshine. Other people are much more willing to toil in the darkness until they find what they're looking for—particularly those leaders whose styles fall on the western side of the model. You're more likely to skip the drudgery and frustration in favor of simply setting out in a new direction.

How to Navigate the Rest of the Book

You've had a chance to read about some of the psychological drivers that may hold you back as a leader, but what about the good stuff? What about the areas where you naturally excel? Chapter 13 in Part 3 is designed to highlight exactly that: the assets that Affirming leaders bring to the team. There you'll find the three lessons that everyone else can learn from leaders like you.

But, of course, other leaders have things to teach you as well. Looking at the model, you may have noticed that the Affirming Dimension is opposite the Resolute Dimension. Chances are that you may need to focus on this dimension, but depending on your individual situation, there may be others that are more important. Next, go to Part 3, where you'll explore the lessons that are most important for you right now.

Chapter 6

The Inclusive Leader

Inclusive leaders have a heightened awareness of the needs of the people around them. And because they have such a rare gift for listening, they're better able to tap into the talents and ideas of members of their team. As a result, they create an environment that's both collaborative and understanding. We'll elaborate on the value of the Inclusive leader in Chapter 14, but in this chapter we want to dig beneath the surface to understand what makes this style of leader tick. More specifically, we want to help Inclusive leaders recognize some of the not-so-obvious psychological factors that can hold them back.

If you're an Inclusive leader, you're probably very patient and accommodating. Through your soft-spoken, gentle demeanor, people recognize that you are genuinely interested in their lives. But clearly, underneath this exterior there are deeper motivations, needs, and assumptions that drive you to act the way you do. The more you understand these drivers, the more you'll be able to consciously control and shape your leadership style.

Based on our research and experience talking to Inclusive

leaders, the qualities listed below may have a significant impact on how you lead.

- A desire to accept
- A desire to surround yourself with the familiar
- A desire to accommodate others
- A tendency to internalize problems
- A desire for harmony
- A lower need for achievement and status

Without a doubt, many of these qualities contribute to some of your most admirable traits as a leader. As we discuss these qualities, however, we'll be focusing a bit more on how they might hold you back in the leadership arena. While you might not identify with all of these qualities, our experience has shown that a number of them probably describe you better than you may initially think.

A Desire to Accept

Leaders with your style often have trouble speaking up about problems, especially if it means criticizing someone else's performance or ideas. You'd much rather go with the flow, and you're probably more comfortable sticking with the status quo than asking questions. Inclusive leaders like you often try to make current ideas work—particularly when the ideas were generated by other people—rather than dealing with the tension of disagreement or uncertainty. You have a tendency to give people the benefit of the doubt, and you don't like having to challenge or confront others.

Because leaders with your style are so agreeable, some people may dismiss your critical thinking abilities, regardless of how sharp they really are. You see, leaders whose styles fall on the western side of the model have a naturally skeptical and questioning nature, whereas leaders like you tend to be warm and accepting. People who see the world through a more critical lens may dismiss your Inclusive approach as too soft, particularly if you don't speak up when things aren't running smoothly or when things seem stagnant.

A Desire to Surround Yourself with the Familiar

Another psychological driver that keeps leaders with your Inclusive approach from embracing change is your comfort with—and preference for—the familiar. Situations that might feel stagnant or too safe to more adventurous leaders tend to be comfortable for leaders like you. In general, Inclusive leaders view predictability as a good thing, and they often build structures and routines that help them avoid chaos or surprises. Change can seem threatening, as it introduces unfamiliar elements and pushes you out of your comfort zone. You tend to see the value of what you already have in front of you, whereas leaders whose styles fall toward the top of the model have a tendency to scan their surroundings constantly for new opportunities. This isn't instinctual for leaders like you, and in fact, you may be reluctant to explore new possibilities that could disrupt your current rhythm. Truthfully, your natural inclination may lean more toward maintaining than leading change.

Don't get us wrong—if a great opportunity falls in your lap, you'll probably explore the possibility, but, because you tend to be absorbed in the safety of the predictable environment that you've built for yourself, you're unlikely to initiate radical change. Sure, you may welcome and even suggest some incremental changes along the way, but generally speaking, leaders with your style focus more energy on minimizing tension and uncertainty. Seeking out fireworks—or the latest-and-greatest idea—doesn't even occur to most Inclusive leaders. Putting out the fires that come up provides plenty of excitement.

A Desire to Accommodate Others

More often than not, Inclusive leaders are eager to meet other people's needs, even if it means adjusting their own plans. Saying "no" can be very difficult for leaders with your style. You have a genuine interest in other people, and you probably show a great deal of empathy for others. While your concern is genuine, you may have a secondary motivation for being empathic: earning affection. Leaders like you may believe you'll be more likeable if you make people feel good about themselves, so you probably do things to show interest in others, such as asking questions and listening carefully.

There are many benefits in being accommodating, but you can also negate your personal authority by taking it too far. There's a tendency for Inclusive leaders to work so hard to protect people's feelings that they come across as wishy-washy, indecisive, or lacking in confidence. In social situations, they may unintentionally give off submissive cues, such as using hesitant language, speaking softly, avoiding eye contact, and trying to make others comfortable by laughing or nodding. Because you're eager to please, you may let others dominate the discussion. Physically, you may have a tendency to make yourself "smaller" with unassertive posture and actions such as looking down and putting your hands in your pockets. Not only do these gestures suggest that you lack confidence, but they also send a message to the other person that they have the power. Interestingly, this desire to minimize yourself not only manifests itself physically, but psychologically as well.

A Tendency to Internalize Problems

Another psychological driver that keeps many Inclusive leaders from embracing their personal authority is their tendency to internalize problems. You'd often rather hold in your frustrations with other people than upset relationships. In fact, you may even blame yourself rather than tell someone that you're unhappy with their performance. If you feel that you've offended someone, it may eat away at you, so you try to avoid such situations at all costs. In particular, you don't want to be seen as overly aggressive, and an unfortunate side effect of this is that others may see you as timid. You probably dislike the idea of having to fight to be heard, but some people may dismiss your input if it's presented with little authority.

Another reason that many Inclusive leaders internalize problems is their fear of drawing out an aggressive response from others. Leaders with your style don't like emotional outbursts, and having someone lash out at you can be quite threatening. In fact, you may have an underlying fear of being cut down in public or of someone calling out your personal flaws. Inclusive leaders like you are slow to anger, so you may have trouble relating to people whose emotions are volatile. Generally speaking, people get angry when they feel that their rights have been violated, but leaders with your style tend to have a diminished view of their own rights. When others become angry with you, you may be quick to see their points of view and assume that their behavior is justified.

A Desire for Harmony

We've already discussed that leaders with your Inclusive approach have a high need for harmony. This is true both in terms of relationships and in tasks. That is, they have an affinity for routines, and they can work tirelessly at a steady rhythm over extended periods of time. We'd be willing to bet that you can turn out remarkably consistent progress day after day—with a smile. You're less likely to get bored with routine than leaders whose approaches fall on the northern side of the model.

Leaders with your Inclusive approach tend to describe themselves as calm and patient, and frankly, you may experience less stress than more hard-charging leaders. On the other hand, your patience can be a problem if it causes you simply to accept your lot when the world—or an individual—doesn't meet your expectations. If you show too much patience, it becomes difficult to set high expectations for others or to instill a sense of urgency. Inclusive leaders may be seen as so focused on harmony that they seem to lack passion. And, in fact, few leaders with your style would describe themselves as having so-called fires in their bellies. They don't have the same intensity and drive that we see in leaders whose approaches fall on the northern side of the model.

At times, leaders have to push the group to work beyond what's comfortable to reach their goals. This involves both initiating action and helping the group maintain momentum. In general, leaders with your style tend to prefer a steady, comfortable pace. They don't like to feel rushed—they'd rather take the time to get things done right. If you consider the 8 Dimensions of Leadership Model, this makes a lot of sense. Remember that those styles on the southern side of the model tend to be cautious and reflective, while those on the northern side are fast-paced and outspoken. Because Inclusive leaders are quite cautious, they tend to process all of the information before acting, and this can cause them to be less responsive to changing environments. When every adjustment of the rudder requires lengthy deliberation, the group becomes less nimble and innovative.

A Lower Need for Achievement and Status

Another psychological driver specific to Inclusive leaders like you is a lower achievement-orientation, especially compared to other leaders. Because your self-esteem is based more on pleasing others and being accepted, you don't see achievement as the most important thing in leadership or in life. In fact, compared to leaders with other styles, you're less likely to strive for high status responsibilities. You probably take a pleasant, laid-back approach to working toward goals, and you may savor the process of getting there. Inclusive leaders like to make sure things move as smoothly as they should, but they aren't anxious to reach the finish line.

Because Inclusive leaders aren't as achievement-oriented, they're less likely to push themselves and others. They tend to see the best in people, and they often trust others to pull their weight. Leaders like you assume that others will work at a responsible pace, and even if you suspect that someone isn't, it may be difficult for you to impose your schedule on them. As we've already discussed, you want to avoid tension, so pushing someone to perform may seem like a risky proposition.

Leaders with your style are often less comfortable with power, so they tend to downplay their own status and defer to others who they see as more charismatic or authoritative. Although it isn't obvious to them, Inclusive leaders can sometimes associate being in a position of superiority over someone as somehow doing that person harm. So, the last thing they want to do is order people around or force them to do things they don't want to do. It's easy to see why Inclusive leaders often try to give away power. In fact, you may have a subconscious urge to make yourself as inconspicuous as possible. By being inconspicuous, you avoid the possibility that someone will call you out as a phony.

Some Inclusive leaders may describe themselves as competitive, but they don't take it personally the way more achievement-oriented leaders do. You probably don't have a desire to put other people in their place, and likewise, you probably don't find it humiliating to be bested by someone else. This is because your ego isn't wrapped up in being number one. This is healthy in many respects, but if taken too far, a lack of competitiveness can pose its own challenges. This is particularly true if you are trying to lead a group of people who happen to be very competitive and driven.

How to Navigate the Rest of the Book

You've had a chance to read about some of the psychological drivers that may hold you back as a leader, but what about the good stuff? What about the areas where you naturally excel? Chapter 14 in Part 3 is designed to highlight exactly that: the assets that Inclusive leaders bring to the table. There you'll find the three lessons that everyone else can learn from leaders like you.

But, of course, other leaders have things to teach you as well. Looking at the model, you may have noticed that the Inclusive Dimension is opposite the Commanding Dimension. Chances are that you may need to focus on this dimension, but depending on your individual situation, there may be others that are more important. Next, go to Part 3, where you'll explore the lessons that are most important for you right now.

Chapter 7

The Humble Leader

More and more leadership experts are beginning to recognize the extremely important role that humility plays in effective leadership. Humble leaders are able to recognize their mistakes, learn from others, give credit where credit is due, maintain their composure, and keep their personal egos in check. We'll elaborate on the value of the Humble leader in Chapter 15, but in this chapter we want to dig beneath the surface to understand what makes this style of leader tick. More specifically, we want to help Humble leaders understand some of the less-than-obvious psychological mechanisms that can hold them back.

If you're a Humble leader, you probably have a bit of a cautious side. You're self-controlled, and people see you as fairly soft-spoken. Underneath this steady exterior there are deeper motivations, needs, and assumptions that drive you to act the way you do. The more you understand these drivers, the more you'll be able to consciously control and shape your leadership style.

Based on our research and experience talking to Humble leaders, the qualities listed below have a significant impact on how you lead.

- A desire to be reliable
- A desire to avoid trouble
- A fear of rocking the boat
- A quality of self-restraint
- A lower level of self-serving ambition
- A desire to be inconspicuous

In many respects, these qualities may lead to some of your greatest strengths as a leader. As we go through these qualities, however, we'll be paying a little more attention to how they might limit your effectiveness. While you might not identify with all of these qualities, our experience has shown that a number of them probably describe you better than you may initially think.

A Desire to Be Reliable

Whereas leaders on the northern side of the model tend to be adventurous, leaders on the southern side want to be seen as steady and reliable. We're willing to bet that you're very conscientious about getting things right the first time, and this is because you don't want to let people down or cause any trouble. Because you don't want to make mistakes that might affect others, you can be prone to inaction. Your responsibility as a leader weighs so heavily on you that you want to plan as thoroughly as possible. You're grateful for the trust that people have in you, and you want to live up to their expectations.

Your desire to be seen as reliable plays a large role in your focus on quality. You like to see things through to closure, and you tend to use established methods that help you execute tasks with precision. If something seems foggy to you, you ask clarifying questions and pursue additional information. Your goal is to have a thorough understanding of each piece of the puzzle. This ensures that you can self-sufficiently control the outcome of your work. There's a certain satisfaction in completing a task to perfection, and wrapping things up in a neat package is gratifying in and of itself. When everything is "just so," you probably feel quite satisfied. Unfortunately, as a leader, focusing too much on closure can also be somewhat of a hindrance in that you may not keep an open mind about trying new methods.

A Desire to Avoid Trouble

One of the main reasons that Humble leaders tend to be big planners is that they want to avoid trouble. Security and stability are high priorities for leaders with your style. Compared to other people, you are much more likely to tolerate a lack of variety. Most of the time, you'd choose to perform tasks that are a little dull over throwing yourself into a chaotic situation. "Safe" settings give you freedom from doubt, anxiety, and unpleasant interpersonal exchanges.

Since you prefer to work in a steady, secure environment, you're probably aware of anything and everything that could go wrong. This means that when presented with a risky situation, you're much more likely to see the potential negative consequences than the positive possibilities. Consider the line that people always say in movies when someone is afraid of heights: "Don't look down." Sometimes, when people see the danger, they become paralyzed with fear. Humble leaders don't just look *down*—they look down, up, left, right, inside, and outside. They want to know exactly how much danger they're up against, and it may stall any forward movement.

Humble leaders don't necessarily trust their intuition when making decisions. Before they feel comfortable moving head, they have to work through all of the known facts and build their decisions with their own logic. At times, they take chances, but only once they have a thorough understanding of the risks. If they're not sure, they delay the gamble to buy themselves more time for research. They want to know more about exactly what type of trouble they may be up against.

A Fear of Rocking the Boat

Because Humble leaders crave consistency, they often try to provide it for others. Given the choice between living in harmony and fighting for what they believe, they are more apt to choose harmony, even if it kills them on the inside. You see, Humble leaders don't want to be the cause of trouble, and they have a strong drive to be free of blame. You may often worry about undefined, nonspecific mistakes that you might have made—even if you can't put a finger on anything specific. You may run through scenarios in your head, checking to make sure that you haven't forgotten something, stepped on someone's toes, or inadvertently botched a task. Because all of this worrying is—well, a lot of *worrying*—you may find that following as many rules as possible helps you to feel like you're minimizing the harm you could be causing.

People with your Humble approach respect rules, both written and self-imposed. On the one hand, showing respect for rules is noble. On the other, rules can also be barriers to positive change. As they say, some rules are made to be broken. Leaders with your approach tend to take comfort in the existence of rules. They provide safety and security. Humble leaders have an unconscious tendency to expand rules to cover areas that they weren't originally intended to cover. At times, you may latch onto assumptions that you see as absolute, when in reality, things may change, and the restrictions may be only in your mind. Leaders with more adventurous approaches challenge assumptions, often seeing something valuable beyond the rules. If they want it bad enough, they find a way to work around the rules to make it happen. It simply may not occur to you to work around the rules.

In our research, three out of five people wanted their Humble leaders to do more to stretch the boundaries. Why is this? Well, if leaders don't see things in a new light—don't wonder what *could be*—their groups aren't likely to evolve. There are some people who no doubt share your preference for peace over stimulation, but there are many more who want to push toward new opportunities. You have some tendencies that lead you to put unnecessary restrictions on yourself, and this can keep you from finding new opportunities and stretching the boundaries.

A Quality of Self-Restraint

Humble leaders are very cautious about expressing their feelings. Although they generally trust other people, they're slow to open up. The idea of expressing their feelings and dreams to another person seems silly or ridiculous, and this may stem from a lack of confidence in the validity of their own inner experience. This is especially true in a work setting, whereas they may be more comfortable sharing their feelings in personal relationships where trust is high. Because Humble leaders filter their thoughts before speaking, it's very rare for them to have emotional outbursts; in fact, they may try to mute the internal experience of emotion. As a consequence, they aren't as likely to be moved by their passions—to get so excited about ideas that they distort reality in favor of their goals. Because they're so grounded and realistic, it can be difficult for Humble leaders to immerse themselves wholeheartedly into an endeavor.

People may not often see your passion, and they also may not see your stress. At times, you may be under a considerable amount of stress, but who would know? You're more likely to ruminate on problems. In fact, it may not even occur to you to express your concerns. It may seem more natural to rely on your own problem-solving abilities. This isn't so much out of pride as it is simply not seeing the purpose of pulling other people into your problems. So, whether you're excited about a new idea, stressed out about a problem, or feeling frustrated, you're likely to keep a pretty even keel. You may not invite others into your emotional landscape, and sometimes this can be interpreted as lacking passion.

Our research has found that the second-highest leadership behavior that Humble leaders are asked to demonstrate more often is "rallying people to achieve goals." You probably do a good job of getting people the resources they need, making sure that polices are in place to get things done, and disseminating information. In a one-on-one context, you may even tend to people's emotional needs by lending a genuine, empathetic ear. But, if you're like most Humble leaders, you may have a much more laissez-faire attitude toward the motivational aspects of leadership. At the heart of this, you may simply doubt your own ability to be a charismatic leader—the kind of person who's good at rallying the troops.

A Lower Level of Self-Serving Ambition

The primary goal of Humble leaders is security, not expansion or control over others. In an ideal world, they work in a comfortable environment where the challenges are just right, but where they ultimately have control over most variables and—perhaps more importantly—they at least *understand* all of the variables. Since their self-esteem isn't based on being superior, they don't typically set grand goals of accomplishment and power. They're willing to let others take the lead without their pride getting in the way. Humble leaders don't want to presume that they're more powerful than anyone else, and this can restrict their action.

As we've discussed, Humble leaders don't want to invite problems, and this makes them more reactive than proactive. While they certainly do react to problems, they are seldom proactive about initiating new opportunities—that's opening a whole new can of (probably messy) worms. If things slow down and you find yourself with some free time, you probably like to straighten up any issues that have been lingering, but you're less likely to muster the internal energy needed to try out a radical new idea. Leaders with your approach both benefit from and suffer from inertia. That is, when you're already in motion, you continue to move steadily along on that path, and this can make you a fantastic contributor. But, when you're at (relative) rest, you may wait for others to initiate change. Regardless of your position in an organization, you may feel that someone above you must *really* be in charge.

A Desire to Be Inconspicuous

OK, we're going to risk getting a little psychoanalytical here in this last section. The issues discussed may seem a little far-fetched at first, but bear with us. In our work with Humble leaders, we've seen a pattern—an unspoken philosophy, probably developed in their youth, that says, "actively engaging in life usually presents more danger than potential." And as a result, many of these leaders harbor a well-hidden, subconscious desire to make themselves inconspicuous—to make themselves small. By being small, they protect themselves from exposure, from the possibility that people will be angry or disappointed with them. There is safety is smallness. The weight of responsibility and pressure is lifted. Being small is the ultimate form of security, and this is a primary goal of Humble leaders. By being unassuming, you can tuck yourself away from the world and its expectations, and more importantly, away from the possibility of failure. Leaders whose styles fall on the northern side of the model have a much higher need to feel important. You're more interested in being free from blame.

While other people often overplay their own rights and opinions, Humble leaders are more likely to underplay them. Humble leaders try to see things fairly, attempting to take their egos out of the equation, and often giving other people the benefit of the doubt. Because you're quick to see the reasonableness of other people's points of view, you often don't push as strongly for your own needs. If someone else promotes an idea with force, you're inclined to say, "Yeah, I can see that, too." Unfortunately, this agreeableness often means that you don't present your ideas with much energy. While this may be ideal in a *fair* world, you're essentially giving others a competitive advantage.

How to Navigate the Rest of the Book

You've had a chance to read about some of the psychological drivers that may hold you back as a leader, but what about the good stuff? What about the areas where you naturally excel? Chapter 15 in Part 3 is designed to highlight exactly that: the assets that Humble leaders bring to the table. There you'll find the three lessons that everyone else can learn from leaders like you.

But, of course, other leaders have things to teach you as well. Looking at the model, you may have noticed that the Humble Dimension is opposite the Pioneering Dimension. Chances are that you may need to focus on this dimension, but depending on your individual situation, there may be others that are more important. Next, go to Part 3, where you'll explore the lessons that are most important for you right now.

Chapter 8

The Deliberate Leader

Deliberate leaders do their homework. They get to the bottom of problems before they propose solutions. And because they take such care to ensure quality, they're able to provide direction that's reliable and well-organized. We'll elaborate on the value of the Deliberate leader in Chapter 16, but in this chapter we want to make a more careful study of this dimension. More specifically, we want to help Deliberate leaders understand some of the subtle and sometimes elusive psychological mechanisms that can hold them back.

If you're a Deliberate leader, you probably have a strong analytical side. Although you tend to be quiet, people have immense respect for your commitment to accuracy. But clearly, underneath this exterior there are deeper motivations, needs, and assumptions that drive you to act the way you do. The more you understand these drivers, the more you'll be able to consciously control and shape your leadership style.

Based on our research and experience talking to Deliberate leaders, the qualities listed below may have a significant impact on how you lead.

- A desire for freedom and privacy
- A reluctance to show emotions
- An innate skepticism of others' ideas
- A distaste for vulnerability
- A desire for objectivity
- A desire for a comfort zone of personal space

Certainly, many of these qualities are directly responsible for your greatest strengths as a leader. As we look at these qualities in more depth, however, we'll be paying a little more attention to some of the ways that they can limit your leadership performance. While you might not identify with all of these qualities, our experience has shown that a number of them probably describe you better than you may initially think.

A Desire for Freedom and Privacy

Many Deliberate leaders don't spend much energy trying to understand the emotional dynamics within the group. In fact, this may feel like a distraction from what you see as your *real* responsibilities. What makes Deliberate leaders shy away from the emotional aspects of leadership? They tend to be private people who like to maintain a bit of personal space, literally and figuratively. Others sometimes describe Deliberate leaders as detached, aloof, or private. Leaders with your approach have a fundamental desire for freedom, both for yourself and others. You may respond poorly to being pressured or coerced into doing something you don't want to do, and you also avoid pressuring other people. To you, that sort of influence feels like showing blatant disrespect for others. However, as a leader, there are many times when it's necessary to put the squeeze on internal and external parties or to simply ask for a favor. Because you hate to bother people, you often avoid such intrusions, and in a competitive world, this can be a liability.

In general, Deliberate leaders aren't the most social people, and this is because social situations tend to be quite unpredictable. You can never guarantee that you'll come across the way you want to when interacting with others—particularly when speaking to new people. You may spend a lot of mental energy focusing your efforts on trying to come across as appropriate. In fact, when other people behave in ways that seem inappropriate to you, you may become embarrassed for them. Whether you know it or not, you probably use a very strong filter when speaking—an effort to maintain your self-control—and this constant monitoring can be exhausting. As a result, you're inclined to minimize the importance of networking and consulting outside your immediate social circle.

A Reluctance to Show Emotions

Another driver that often prevents Deliberate leaders from attending to the emotional aspects of leadership is that they tend to be quite matter-of-fact. Though you're normally reserved, you probably don't have a problem speaking up when you see or hear something that seems illogical to you. In fact, half-baked ideas may strike you as a personal assault, and you may call attention to them in ways that seem insensitive to others. Your mind is very attuned to getting the job done and remaining objective. It may take you by surprise when you learn that you've hurt someone's feelings. You make sure that everyone is treated fairly, but you're not often able to put yourself in the emotional shoes of other people.

Deliberate leaders often have trouble recognizing other people's emotional needs, and as a result of this, they don't give praise readily. They may not realize it, but some people probably interpret their silence as disapproval. Most Deliberate leaders simply don't grasp that some people have a high need for praise. Rather, you may believe that being correct or doing a good job is its own reward. Subconsciously, you may feel that delivering praise creates a level of intimacy that makes you uncomfortable. With the exception of your close friends and family, you'd often rather keep some emotional distance from others. The idea of showering people with praise and compliments may even make you feel a little squeamish.

Because leaders like you tend to be matter-of-fact, you may struggle with emotional appeals, both in terms of making them *and* being on the receiving end. You're much more concerned with logic, and you want to be sure that the idea is a good one, not just that the *pitch* is a good one. Doing anything other than following the most logical course of action feels dishonest to Deliberate leaders. Their credibility is very important to them, so when other people come to them with emotional appeals, they're likely to take a skeptical stance. When you're in a position to sell an idea to a group, you'd probably be hard-pressed to come up with a compelling emotional argument for something that you didn't believe in.

An Innate Skepticism of Others' Ideas

Why, exactly, do good ideas sometimes scare leaders like you? Simply put, you want to have control. Other leadership dimensions revolve around control, but in a different sense. Commanding leaders seek to control the environment and to be recognized as being in control. You're more likely to want to control the quality of your work. You have a core belief that you should not be wrong—it's almost a moral imperative to leaders like you that you be right. Being associated with shoddy work or bad ideas is probably your worst nightmare as a leader. It's natural, then, that you bring a good deal of skepticism to the table when you hear other people's ideas. If you're going to put your good name on an idea, a service, or a product, it must be of the highest quality.

Not only are Deliberate leaders skeptical of other people's ideas, but they can also be quite stubborn. Expertise is extremely important to them—in fact, it plays a huge part in how they develop and maintain their feelings of self-worth—so admitting that they're wrong is extremely difficult. Showing expertise gives leaders like you the chance to be on the offensive rather than the defensive. It's a chance to have a sense of pride. Whereas others have their pride needs met by winning or getting attention, Deliberate leaders have them met through credibility. They often assume that their logic is best, and it may be difficult for them to realize that two logical people can reach very different conclusions. They may underestimate the role that values, experience, and self-interest play as people—themselves included—form opinions.

A Distaste for Vulnerability

Deliberate leaders have a fundamental fear of being vulnerable, and this can cause them to shy away from seemingly risky ideas. You probably don't like to put yourself out there. You're inherently cautious, and this allows you to ensure accuracy as much as possible. You often want to have a potentially unrealistic level of certainty before you make a decision. Sure, everyone wants some certainty of success before taking a chance, but this threshold is particularly high for Deliberate leaders. This often causes you to avoid risks altogether, or even to fail to acknowledge opportunities. Whether it's in a social setting or in a professional setting, you're unlikely to stick your neck out unless you're quite sure of the outcome.

Where does this hesitancy come from? Deliberate leaders like you tend to be anxious about flaws—a base fear that someone might see the *real* you with all your imperfections. You may push these fears out of your mind, but subconsciously, they're always there. Below the surface, you're afraid of being exposed, of having horrible flaws spill out that will humiliate you or make you unlovable. Most Deliberate leaders hide these insecurities, even to themselves, because they see them as a mark against their competency. They're careful not to show weakness to others, especially in areas that they think matter. If they find themselves in a vulnerable position, they're likely to go off on their own to do research or try to solve the problem. Leaders like you want to have a high degree of self-control. You can't always control your environment, but you can control yourself. In this way, you can avoid making a fool of yourself.

A Desire for Objectivity

What makes Deliberate leaders so sure of their own logic? You probably consider yourself objective—and you often are—but everyone brings their own biases to the table. In fact, you may have a bias toward things that are logical and predictable. For example, you may think that emotional considerations don't matter in a leadership context. Sure, emotions are a natural part of life, but you probably don't see them as a valid part of the decision-making process. Likewise, you may be disgusted when people's political motives influence the course of events. Many Deliberate leaders refuse to get involved in organizational politics, which they consider silly, irrational, or manipulative. You may get frustrated when people seem swayed by politics or emotion over reason, and you're very unlikely to use these tactics yourself.

Because leaders like you find beauty and elegance in logical arguments, problem solving may be highly emotionally satisfying to you. You may enjoy sorting through chaos to find an elegant order or working through a process to find the correct answer. In the same way that socializing is gratifying to Energizing leaders, your brain is wired to find gratification in solving problems. When you're fully immersed in the game of figuring out a problem, the pleasure centers of your brain light up and you can taste the reward—the answer—hiding just around the corner.

As a Deliberate leader, you may have trouble seeing beyond your own logic, and as a result, you may often stay on a path that makes sense on paper, even when it doesn't align with more dynamic, unpredictable variables of the real world. The danger in this, of course, is leading a team or an organization that doesn't keep up with the demands of the fast-moving world. When dealing with other people, you may fail to recognize that alternative streams of logic can be every bit as valid as yours. Rather, you may assume that people whose opinions differ from your own simply don't get it.

A Desire for a Comfort Zone of Personal Space

Deliberate leaders often isolate themselves. We've mentioned that leaders like you tend to stay in their comfort zones, and you may even create a protective bubble around yourself. When other people try to invade your space, you may feel some discomfort, if only subconsciously. It may require a lot of energy for you to let other people have access to your space, whether it be physical, intellectual, or emotional. For leaders who are more people-oriented, this requires very little emotional energy. In fact, they find it energizing. Because making interpersonal connections can be a lot of work for you, you may come across as standoffish or distant. Your desire to stay in your bubble has important implications for where you take—or don't take—groups that you lead. In general, many Deliberate leaders keep their groups in familiar territory, limiting opportunities that involve stretching beyond the group's known competencies.

Why this isolation? Deliberate leaders enjoy getting immersed in solving a problem so much that they create the space they need to avoid interference from the outside world. Social tasks like making phone calls often get put off. Now, we're not saying that you don't *sometimes* like to have people around, because we're sure that you do, but compared to other leaders, you require more personal space. Individual tasks that require a lot of analytical brainpower are really fun for you, and you may easily get lost in activities such as working on a spreadsheet, playing a computer game, figuring out a puzzle, or crafting an essay. When you're engaged in an activity like this, you may tune other people out, and even if you get stuck, you're unlikely to ask for help. Not only do you not want to bother people, but you like the challenge of trying to master a problem on your own. There's nothing wrong with independence, but when you isolate yourself too much, you fail to take stock of what's happening in the world around you.

Further, Deliberate leaders gravitate toward stable environments where there's plenty of time to gather information and make well-informed decisions. Of course, stability has its own merits, but if it's not balanced with some element of risk-taking, it's tough for an organization to be competitive. Because Deliberate leaders have a strong need to control the variables, they tend to keep their group within known, comfortable parameters. Sure, they're sometimes willing to learn new things and take on tough challenges, but it's usually within domains that they're confident they can conquer. Wildcard variables make them nervous—they're much more comfortable building slowly on what's been done in the past. So Deliberate leaders *do* move forward, but only when they can see for themselves how every dot connects with the others.

How to Navigate the Rest of the Book

You've had a chance to read about some of the psychological drivers that may hold you back as a leader, but what about the good stuff? What about the areas where you naturally thrive? Chapter 16 in Part 3 is designed to highlight just that: the strengths that Deliberate leaders bring to the group. There you'll find the three lessons that everyone else can learn from leaders like you.

But, of course, other leaders have things to teach you as well. Looking at the model, you may have noticed that the Deliberate Dimension is opposite the Energizing Dimension. Chances are that you may need to focus on this dimension, but depending on your individual situation, there may be others that are more important. Next, go to Part 3, where you'll explore the lessons that are most important for you right now.

Chapter 9

The Resolute Leader

As the name suggests, Resolute leaders are highly determined. Their strong-willed persistence and their inner strength give people the courage to get though tough times. We'll elaborate on the value of the Resolute leader in Chapter 17, but in this chapter we want to dig beneath the surface to understand what makes this style of leader tick. More specifically, we want to help Resolute leaders recognize some of the sometimes hidden psychological mechanisms that can hold them back.

If you're a Resolute leader, you may have a bit of a questioning side. There's a no-nonsense quality to your leadership, and people probably respect your willingness to speak up about problems. But beneath this tough exterior are deeper motivations, needs, and assumptions that drive you to act the way you do. The more you understand these drivers, the more you'll be able to consciously control and shape your leadership style.

Based on our research and experience talking to Resolute leaders, the qualities listed below may have a significant impact on how you lead.

- A natural skepticism
- A drive toward personal mastery

- A tenacious drive to overcome obstacles
- A predisposition toward disgust
- A disdain for weakness
- An over-reliance on "should"

We have no doubt that many of these qualities contribute to some of your most compelling strengths as a leader. As we go through these qualities in more depth, however, the emphasis will be on the potential limitations caused by these same attributes. While you might not identify with all of these qualities, our experience has shown that a number of them probably describe you better than you may initially think.

A Natural Skepticism

Resolute leaders have a natural skepticism that can make them less attentive to team dynamics. You probably pride yourself on your critical thinking ability, and after a lifetime of asking challenging questions, you may not have developed the nonverbal behaviors that send encouraging messages to others such as smiling, politely laughing at a joke, or nodding. When you first meet people, you have a "wait and see" attitude. Because of your skepticism, you may come across as disinterested or guarded. To put it another way, you may not have a particularly open or trusting attitude toward other people. Michele, a Resolute human resources director in the insurance industry, put it this way, "When I first meet people—I'm very serious in most business situations—I start out serious. I can be pretty funny sometimes, but not in the beginning."

Not only are Resolute leaders skeptical, but they often feel the need to voice their concerns. They may feel like they have no choice—when their standards are violated, they take it very personally. This is one of the ways that Resolute leaders gain a sense of power. You may find that when you push others to prove themselves, many of them rise to the occasion, especially when they have a high need for approval. This allows you to drive the relationship. By establishing your high standards, you define what is important. While many people will respond to your high standards by trying to meet them, a few may be turned off by your aggressiveness. Either way, the other party may not feel entirely comfortable with you. Because they probably see you as strong, they may follow you, but often at a safe distance.

A Drive toward Personal Mastery

Resolute leaders have a strong drive to control the world around them, to have some influence on the variables that affect them. More than anything, they want to understand these variables, so they work to develop their own set of principles about how the world works. What they don't realize is that this is not necessarily how the world *actually* works, but they attach a lot of "shoulds" to their own outlook on life. People *should* work a certain way, projects *should* be managed a certain way, and businesses *should* be run—you got it—a *certain way*. Resolute leaders put so much effort into understanding and organizing the world around them because, above all else, they feel a strong internal need to be competent.

Not only do Resolute leaders expect themselves to be competent, but they have very little patience for other people who they regard as incompetent. If they must work with people who they see as less able, Resolute leaders have a tendency to work around them. For example, Resolute leaders may give them minimal responsibility, not include them on updates, and simply not utilize them. Rather than making an effort to fully engage them and discover their passions and talents, they may dismiss them entirely. When people who seem incompetent share their ideas with you, how do you respond? All too often, Resolute leaders express subtle disdain or simply don't listen.

Leaders with your approach have extremely high standards. When things go well, you may not be too terribly impressed— you expect the best. However, when things go wrong, your disapproval may be clear. Unfortunately, if you only react when things don't work out, you create an environment where only mistakes are recognized. People may find this both intimidating and demoralizing, and it can cause them to focus more on avoiding mistakes than on really pushing themselves to stretch and grow.

A Tenacious Drive to Overcome Obstacles

Resolute leaders have a strong need for personal mastery. From early on, they have an inherent belief that they need to have control over their lives. This allows for self-sufficiency and (hopefully) guards them from the humiliation of incompetence. Leaders like you tend to build their self-worth on mastery and competency. If you feel that you're competent, you feel like a worthy person. Because this is so wrapped up in your personal identity, you home in on exactly what you want and put your passion and energy behind it until it's achieved. You can be very single-minded when you're working toward a goal, and you're willing to push through all manner of discomfort to gain mastery. This is one of the benefits of being comfortable with negative emotion. Where others might say "To heck with this," you're willing to persist.

Resolute leaders also genuinely enjoy solving problems, and they don't mind wrestling with ambiguity. In your lifetime, you've probably received strong positive reinforcement—both internal and external—for coming up with solutions to tricky problems. On the flip side, you've probably also experienced extreme discomfort in situations where you can't figure out a problem. Some people may be able to shake off such disappointment and move on, but it often really vexes Resolute leaders. It feels unsettling to not resolve the problem, so leaders like you often just keep pushing.

Although Resolute leaders are motivated by solving problems and overcoming barriers, other people aren't built that way—and it's not because they're broken. Many people need to feel excited about goals and to feel that their contributions are recognized. You may have difficulty generating enthusiasm and doling out praise because you're naturally skeptical of emotional appeals. You don't tend to give any rah-rah speeches, and you may resent the idea that anyone expects them from you. You want to keep things logical and professional, and you may feel that there's something vaguely unprofessional about enthusiasm. Rather, you often stick to a more hard-nosed, down-to-business approach. In your mind, that's your job as a leader.

A Predisposition toward Disgust

Resolute leaders are often vigorous debaters, even if it's just playing out an argument in their head. Using reason and ingenuity, they enjoy finding the flaws in another person's argument and pulling it apart. On the surface, this might seem to be just a cognitive exercise. In reality, however, it's just as much about emotion as logic. And what's the dominant emotion present when we engage in debate? MRI studies have found that different parts of the brain light up during debate (Westen et al, 2006). Not surprisingly, the prefrontal cortex is active, which is associated with complex cognition. But, interestingly, another part of the brain is also often active: the part associated with disgust.

New research is also discovering a surprising link between many negative emotions and pleasure. Emotions can be addictive. We've all heard the phrases, "wallowing in sadness" or "stewing in anger." *Wallowing* in sadness or *stewing* in anger leads to a spike in pleasure, but then leaves the individual feeling worse than before. So the person chases the negative emotion again, and a cognitive pattern develops. Because thoughts are more subtle than drugs or gambling or shopping, it's difficult to recognize this type of pattern, and it's even more difficult to stop. Without realizing it consciously, those with the Resolute style often learn how pleasurable being disgusted can feel and go back to this emotion again and again. You may believe that you have no choice but to be disgusted because the errors of another person are so egregious. Perhaps their logic is unforgivably flawed or their actions are inexcusably self-serving. If there is a reason to be disgusted with someone's behavior, the Resolute leader has a talent for finding it.

Many Resolute leaders have developed a tough shell to manage their discomfort with vulnerability. When pressed, experienced Resolute leaders often reluctantly acknowledge that early on in their careers, they projected their underlying frustration on other things and people. They used to tell themselves that they had no choice but to be disgusted, but they now realize that they were looking for excuses to be outraged. When Resolute leaders get angry, they aren't often explosive, but they can give off a number of nonverbal signals that can be intimidating. Their actions send messages such as, "Don't waste my time," "Are you kidding me?" or "I'm not buying it." We all have social needs, and for many people, gaining approval or admiration is among them. For Resolute leaders like you, it's to maintain respect. For this reason, you're not as concerned with giving off cues that say, "Like me."

A Disdain for Weakness

Resolute leaders generally have little tolerance for personal weakness. While they hold others to high standards, they may be even more ruthless toward themselves. Because they see being emotional as being weak, they often describe themselves as unsentimental. Unconsciously, you may distance yourself from others to avoid intimacy, particularly in a professional setting. Throughout your life, you may have detached yourself both to ensure order in your world and to protect yourself from being hurt. Even if you're sometimes able to let your guard down, traces of this fundamental detachment may linger. When leading others, this can pose a challenge. It's difficult to rally the troops if you don't have a strong connection with the people.

Because you have a tendency to be detached, you may see what some would call "generating enthusiasm" as coddling. You may be put off by the idea of enabling people who won't motivate themselves. Because you're able to set your own goals and keep yourself on track, you may think that everyone should have the ability to do so. When people don't carry their own weight, you may think it's not only unfair, but it's insulting. When people are wallowing in sadness, helplessness, or self-pity, many leaders want to help them work through their issues. You may have a different perspective. Your gut reaction may be utter disgust at their weakness, self-absorption, and selfishness. Truth be told, you have little respect for the role that emotions play in a person's ability to perform. You are used to pushing aside your own emotions to get the job done. It may be difficult for you to empathize with feelings like helplessness, because you're more of the mentality that people should pull themselves up by their bootstraps.

An Over-Reliance on "Should"

Resolute leaders often have a clear sense of how things should go. They've built their views on logic and analysis. Subconsciously, you may want people to play by your rules (i.e., the *right* rules), and you may feel underlying irritation toward anyone who chooses not to. And because others have so frequently gotten it wrong, you may often feel like a team of one. Relying on others—especially those who haven't proven themselves—is difficult. In fact, it may be a comfort to you when the only true obstacle standing between you and your goals is your own effort. When you have to trust others, you don't have this control, but you still want it. When people aren't amenable to your attempts to get them to do things the "right" way, it's probably really frustrating for you. Part of you is tempted to say, "Forget it—I'll do it myself." As a leader, you have to accept that you can't always get people to do things to your exact standards.

You probably have strong opinions about how things *should* be done. It may be very difficult for you to relate to those who see things differently than you, and you may often feel that you could do things more efficiently than most people. You want to balance quality with speed, and it may be frustrating to watch people who don't share these values. Your opinions on how things should be done are also built on your own bias toward logic, particularly *your* logic. Once you've worked through the logic of an idea and feel confident in it, it's very difficult to change your mind. After building a list of solid reasons for your opinions, they become your vision, which you come to think of as fair and objective. What you may not realize is just how much your opinions are actually influenced by your individual experiences and values.

How to Navigate the Rest of the Book

You've had a chance to read about some of the psychological drivers that may hold you back as a leader, but what about the positive stuff? What about the areas where you naturally thrive? Chapter 17 in Part 3 is designed to highlight just that: the assets that Resolute leaders bring to leadership. There you'll find the three lessons that everyone else can learn from leaders like you.

But, of course, other leaders have things to teach you as well. Looking at the model, you may have noticed that the Resolute Dimension is opposite the Affirming Dimension. Chances are that you may need to focus on this dimension, but depending on your individual situation, there may be others that are more important. Next, go to Part 3, where you'll explore the lessons that are most important for you right now.

Chapter 10

The Commanding Leader

When we speak of leadership, the Commanding leader is often the first image that comes to mind. These leaders are decisive and direct. They take charge of the situation and show a rare level of confidence. We'll elaborate on the value of the Commanding leader in Chapter 18, but in this chapter we want to delve beneath the surface to understand what drives this style of leader. More specifically, we want to help Commanding leaders understand some of the more subtle psychological mechanisms that tend to cause them problems in the long run.

If you're a Commanding leader, you probably have a fairly dominant presence. You call it like you see it and can be forceful to get what you want. Underneath this tough outer shell are deeper motivations, needs, and assumptions that drive you to act the way you do. The more you understand these drivers, the more you'll be able to consciously control and shape your leadership style.

Based on our research and experience talking to Commanding leaders, the qualities listed below have a significant impact on how you lead.

- Subjective realism
- A need for triumph
- A high need for achievement
- A disgust for "soft" emotions
- Tough-mindedness
- A drive to move forward quickly

In many respects, these qualities can be a great asset for you. As we go through these qualities, however, we'll be focusing more on how they might limit your effectiveness. While you might not identify with all of these qualities, our experience has shown that a number of them probably describe you better than you may initially think.

Subjective Realism

To maintain their high-speed drive to achieve, Commanding leaders like you rely on a high degree of confidence. Because they've trained themselves to believe in their own abilities, they can be slow to recognize the errors of their own ways. Once they make a decision, they bury any pesky doubts that may start to surface, and this can leave them with an unrealistic confidence in their ideas and decisions. In general, Commanding leaders tend to latch onto specific ideas—usually their own—and they often lack patience for any ideas that contradict them. Because they see their visions so clearly in their own minds, they may assume that those who disagree simply lack the necessary insight.

Perhaps you're aware that some people view you as arrogant, but you probably brush this aside, assuming that others don't understand the "real" state of affairs. Leaders with your style often consider themselves to be uncompromising realists. They don't adjust their perceptions to make the world seem nicer. In fact, you may feel that you see things for what they *really* are, and that anyone who sees things differently is probably just blinded by stupidity, insecurity, or a silly adherence to social conventions like politeness.

Subjective realism often causes Commanding leaders to point out the flaws and inconsistencies in other people's ideas and arguments. As we discussed in Chapter 2, leaders with your style tend to be questioning and skeptical, and this can be hard on warm and accepting people who fall on the eastern side of the model. When giving feedback, you may focus on the challenge of finding flaws without considering the impact of your words on the other person. However, most Commanding leaders don't see things quite the same way when the tables are turned. In fact, leaders like you often take criticism quite poorly. Though they see giving criticism as doling out realism, they may feel that it's a great injustice when others dissect their own work and ideas.

Commanding leaders' inflated sense of power can also close them off to outside input. If fact, power can have this effect on most of us. In a recent study (Brinol et al., 2007), researchers separated participants into two groups. One group of participants was made to feel more powerful and the other made to feel less powerful. The researchers then looked to see how these participants reacted to outside persuasion. As expected, participants in the "low-power" condition reacted favorably to strong arguments and unfavorably to weak arguments. Participants in the "high-power" condition, however, reacted unfavorably to both strong and weak arguments. In other words, their opinions couldn't be influenced no matter how strong an outside argument was. Now, many Commanding leaders, seeing themselves as powerful, may view this as a sign of strength, but to put it bluntly, it's not. It's an Achilles' heal. Because you are naturally imbued with an outward sense of power and self-confidence you need to be extra careful that you do not close yourself off to the feedback that the outside world is trying to give you.

A Need for Triumph

Subconsciously, Commanding leaders may believe that it's not enough just to win, but others must also fail, hence underscoring their superiority. The idea that other people might have ideas that compete against their own may even feel like an insult. When others try to contradict you, you may often put them in their place. Because you have a lot at stake when it comes to competition—essentially, your self-esteem—you often size up other people's strengths and weaknesses, much like an athletic coach scouts upcoming opponents. You may even try to intimidate or bully others into submission. Commanding leaders have an above-average ability to tolerate conflict, and you may sometimes use this to your advantage, slowly wearing down others who can't handle as much emotional strife.

In fact, leaders with your Commanding approach often gain some satisfaction from conflict. A battle of rapid-fire ideas may fuel your competitiveness, and you may experience a sort of euphoria in the heat of the moment. No matter the topic, Commanding leaders fight tenaciously for their viewpoints, and if they feel that they're pinned against the wall, they may become quite aggressive because of their win-at-all-costs instincts. When asked, these leaders claim that they are aggressive because they *have* to be. They point to outside circumstances that require them to be aggressive (e.g., other people are being selfish, irrational, or just plain stupid). They have no choice.

Research, however, suggests that this may not be entirely accurate. Those who use aggression have a secondary motivation: pleasure. A recent study suggests that the brain rewards aggression with dopamine much the same way it rewards food, sex, and drugs (Couppis & Kennedy, 2008). Like other highly rewarded behaviors, we can grow to overuse aggression because the allure of pleasure is so great. If Commanding leaders are honest with themselves, they are often forced to admit that they push forward on conflicts not because they *have* to, but rather because there is a disguised sense of pleasure working in the background.

Because they want to come out on top, Commanding leaders often have trouble working with those they see as arrogant. In fact, you may butt heads in particular with other Commanding leaders. In special cases, you may admire and respect confident people, but if your ego is threatened, you're more likely to view self-assured people with contempt. An unfortunate side effect is that you may cut down the people you work with to make sure they don't get too full of themselves. Leaders like you may convince yourselves that it's for their own good, but in reality, you're just trying to put them in their place, and this can be incredibly frustrating for others.

A High Need for Achievement

Commanding leaders often pride themselves on being able to pull themselves up by their bootstraps. Because they tend to assume that nobody will take care of their needs for them, they take control themselves. Not only do Commanding leaders impose this self-reliance on themselves, but they may expect others to have a similar level of self-sufficiency. Generally speaking, those on the western side of the model often share this more autonomous mindset, while those on the eastern side often think more collaboratively. Commanding leaders may lose patience with people who seem to need a lot of hand-holding or who don't understand things that seem obvious. In fact, leaders with your style may sometimes act as though they could complete everyone's work, with better results, if only they had the time. Chances are, you're intensely competitive, and this can cause you to view yourself as a team of one. On a subconscious level, you may feel driven to succeed entirely on your own as a matter of personal pride.

Given their individualism and high standards, Commanding leaders like you often fail to recognize the contributions of others. And, even when you do give some form of recognition, the bar is set pretty high. You may believe that giving praise for anything less than a spectacular breakthrough is simply coddling. Why do you have such high standards for others? Most likely, it starts with having high standards for yourself.

Leaders with your Commanding approach often have a nagging sense that they must keep moving—a self-imposed obligation to "earn their keep." This assumption is so deep-seated that they may not fully grasp that others legitimately see the world differently. To you, a constant pressure to perform seems akin to breathing. To be sure, this mindset has some impressive implications in the realm of leadership, but it may also create a tendency to take credit for successes. Because Commanding leaders have a confident, goal-oriented leadership style, you may naturally focus on the role *you* played in contributing to a successful outcome.

A Disgust for "Soft" Emotions

Commanding leaders are naturally attracted to emotions that reflect power—most notably, passion and anger. Through passion, you have the power to inspire others, and through anger, to intimidate. When you see other people display more tender emotions such as sadness, affection, or fear, you may sometimes see them as overly sentimental, gushy, or wimpy. And you may feel forced—or at least pressured—to have an empathic response. Subconsciously, you may even feel that you're being manipulated into expressing an emotion that is the epitome of what you despise: weakness and vulnerability.

On a practical level, this aversion to tenderness has some consequences. For instance, you may be uncomfortable giving praise to others, and even a modest compliment may feel like gushing. On a subconscious level, you may feel that praising others can blur the lines between the professional and the intimate. In short, giving praise can make you feel squeamish unless it's done in a rugged, emotionally sanitized manner. Ultimately, this means that you may be very slow to give out praise or recognition, and when you do, it may be terse and objective.

Tough-Mindedness

If you're familiar with *The Sopranos,* the HBO series about a modern crime family, you probably know that its cast is Commanding through and through. As a group, they create a culture with no tolerance for weakness. If someone doesn't assert their strength, they're on their way out—really *out* in the worst sense. Viewers get a fascinating look into this mindset as the patriarch, Tony Soprano, is forced to seek therapy, the ultimate form of mental weakness in the eyes of those who long to be in control. He lashes out at the therapist, seeks to manipulate her, and even tries to seduce her—anything to maintain power in what he undoubtedly sees as a compromised position. In fact, opening himself up in therapy is probably more threatening to him than any violence he might encounter out on the street.

Now, keep in mind that Tony is an extreme version of a Commanding leader, but he illustrates an important aspect of the Commanding mindset. Very often, leaders with your approach have a strong—usually unspoken—aversion to personal vulnerability or weakness. And for most Commanding leaders, it's an aversion that's learned very early on. The result of this aversion to vulnerability is that Commanding leaders often maintain a tough exterior. To others, you may seem a little rough around the edges, and you may say things that seem harsh.

Leaders with your Commanding approach often bring a great deal of intensity to their work. Most of the time, leaders like you are aware that they have a certain edginess. However, quite often, they vastly underestimate the impact that their intensity has on other people. For instance, your words and actions may seem fairly harmless in your own mind, but to others, they can come across as combative or demoralizing. When people perceive that you are indifferent or even hostile toward them, it can erode loyalty to both you as a leader and the organization.

A Drive to Move Forward Quickly

Because Commanding leaders are so driven to accomplish, they also tend to be impatient. We know one leader who proudly hung a sign in her office that read, "Impatience is a virtue." And in many respects, it is—one of a leader's most important jobs is to instill a sense of urgency in the group, and this is a natural role for Commanding leaders to play. However, this heightened eagerness is often accompanied by frustration. The leader is likely to become frustrated when her expectations aren't met, and this can be unhealthy for both the leader and those around her. Compared to others, leaders with your style tend to have very strong stress responses when things don't go their way. You may experience a much greater increase in blood pressure and muscle tension compared to others.

Leaders like you often have to work hard to control how much of their frustration they show. At the same time, the people around you can almost always sense more of your frustration than you think. You may feel that your frustration isn't really anyone's business, but people make it their business; it's human nature. When leaders are prone to frustration, it's extremely stressful for those working with them. In our research, Commanding leaders were the ones who were most often asked to do a better job of maintaining their composure. Simply put, the people who work with Commanding leaders often see them as capable of creating an emotionally unpredictable environment where people are motivated by fear rather than passion.

How to Navigate the Rest of the Book

You've had a chance to read about some of the psychological drivers that may hold you back as a leader, but what about the positive stuff? What about the areas where you naturally excel? Chapter 18 in Part 3 is designed to highlight exactly that: the assets that Commanding leaders bring to the table. There you'll find the three lessons that everyone else can learn from leaders like you.

But, of course, other leaders have things to teach you as well. Looking at the model, you may have noticed that the Commanding Dimension is opposite the Inclusive Dimension. Chances are that you may need to focus on this dimension, but depending on your individual situation, there may be others that are more important. Next, go to Part 3, where you'll explore the lessons that are most important for you right now.

Part 3
Lessons From the 8 Dimensions

Now that you've had a chance to take a deeper dive into your primary leadership dimension and explore some of the psychological drivers that not only help you succeed but also hold you back, the question still remains: What should you do about it? You have an exciting opportunity to broaden your reach as a leader by exploring the benefits of the other seven dimensions. As we talked to leaders during our research, we asked them to describe who or what helped them to develop. As you might expect, many of them described the simple process of trial and error. For some, there was what psychologists call a "peak experience," in which a uniquely powerful situation helped them see something they had been missing. But quite often, leaders attributed their most significant growth to the influence of important role models.

In the course of our careers, we often have the privilege of working with people who exemplify a particular leadership dimension. We admire them because they are such masters that they can easily navigate situations that we dread. They have so deeply absorbed the strengths of a particular leadership dimension that they can achieve certain results by what seems like magic. In each chapter of Part 3, you'll learn specific, research-based lessons from eight archetypical leaders who each embody a particular dimension and can demonstrate its benefits. In real life, we aren't always lucky enough to come across the right mentor or role model at the right time, but the wisdom distilled in these chapters can serve as a strong surrogate for you as you strive to work on specific dimensions to increase your effectiveness.

While it would be fantastic to develop all seven dimensions simultaneously, this is not realistic. So, where do you start? Well, many leaders find that they need to develop the dimension that sits opposite their own primary dimension on the model. For example, Pioneering leaders often need to learn something from Humble leaders. However, our research also shows that the most important dimension for you to work on today also depends on your current role, the culture of your organization, and your personal goals. You may even wish to take external feedback into account. You're the best judge of what skills you need right now. To help you organize your thoughts, take a couple of minutes to fill out the 8 Dimensions of Leadership Needs Assessment below. If you've already completed the online assessment, you can skip the next two pages. Your results for this needs assessment are included on the one-page document you received.

The 8 Dimensions of Leadership Needs Assessment

This simple exercise—separate from your DiSC® assessment—is meant to help you discover the most important dimensions for you to work on today.

Instructions: For each block of four statements, choose the leadership skill that **you most need to improve on** to be more effective as a leader and put a **10** in the corresponding box to the right. Then, choose a runner-up and put a **5** in the corresponding box. (Each set of four should total 15.)

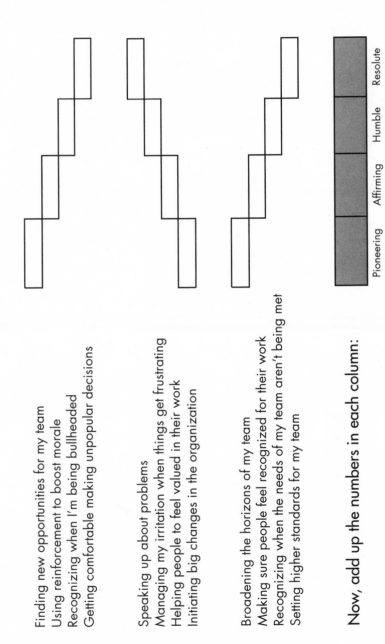

Finding new opportunities for my team
Using reinforcement to boost morale
Recognizing when I'm being bullheaded
Getting comfortable making unpopular decisions

Speaking up about problems
Managing my irritation when things get frustrating
Helping people to feel valued in their work
Initiating big changes in the organization

Broadening the horizons of my team
Making sure people feel recognized for their work
Recognizing when the needs of my team aren't being met
Setting higher standards for my team

Now, add up the numbers in each column:

Continued on the next page.

Leadership Needs Assessment (continued)
Please follow the instructions from the previous page:

Getting people excited about new goals
Listening with more depth to the people on my team
Being thorough and clear in my communication
Focusing my team on results

Stepping up to take charge
Developing more efficient processes and systems
Showing people that I'm open to their ideas
Creating enthusiasm among my team

Building a larger professional network
Making sure that everyone feels that their voice has been heard
Completing a disciplined analysis before making a decision
Creating a greater sense of urgency on my team

Now, add up the numbers in each column:

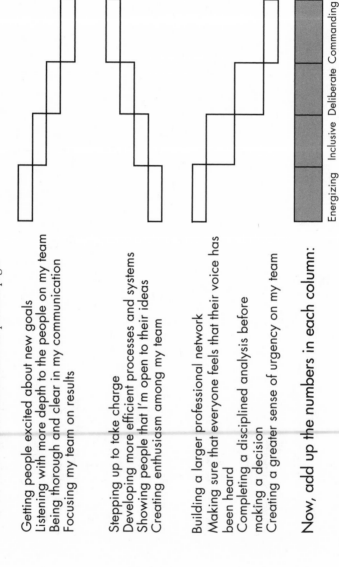

Energizing   Inclusive   Deliberate   Commanding

And now that you've finished the assessment:

1. Look at the eight shaded boxes and circle the two that are highest.
2. Turn to the chapters in Part 3 that explore each of those leadership dimensions.
3. Read specific lessons from each dimension that you've selected.
4. Wrap up your experience by reading Chapter 19: Pulling it All Together.

This development process isn't a one-time thing. Our hope is that you will revisit this book many times throughout the course of your career. Ultimately, each of the chapters in Part 3 has something to reveal to you. In fact, it's important to take some time to celebrate your own unique approach to leadership. You've got a lot to teach others, and we encourage you to read the chapter about your primary dimension so that you can appreciate the natural talent that you already bring to the table.

If you want to work on:	Turn to:
Pioneering:	Chapter 11
Energizing:	Chapter 12
Affirming:	Chapter 13
Inclusive:	Chapter 14
Humble:	Chapter 15
Deliberate:	Chapter 16
Resolute:	Chapter 17
Commanding:	Chapter 18

Chapter 11

Lessons from Pioneering Leaders

What Can We Learn from Pioneering Leaders?

Pioneering leaders are often aggressive about taking risks, and our research suggests that this is an area of leadership that many people wish they'd done more of earlier in their careers. Whether you consider yourself high or low on the Pioneering Dimension, we'll show you the ins and outs of this dynamic approach. As we discussed in Chapter 2, the Pioneering Dimension is located on the northern side of the model, which means that Pioneering leaders tend to be fast-paced and outspoken. We'll explore some key characteristics that epitomize the Pioneering Dimension of leadership in action.

Pioneering leaders want to drive the group toward results, to share their passion and energy, and more than anything, to keep things moving onward and upward at a rapid pace. These achievement-oriented leaders exude an air of confidence and authority, and they tend to set lofty goals for both themselves and the group. They see themselves as inspirational, and they often enjoy the challenge of rallying people together to work toward a shared vision. They're charismatic leaders who work hard to gain alignment with the people they need to get the job done. Like other leaders whose styles fall on the northern side of the model, Pioneering leaders like to maintain a fast pace. These leaders are particularly willing to take risks, to seek out new opportunities, and to make rapid changes.

There are many benefits to the Pioneering Dimension. These leaders have a self-starting capability that stems from their strong sense of vision and their tendency to take initiative. They're drawn to adventurous new ideas, and they often create an environment where creativity is encouraged. Pioneering leaders are high-energy folks, and they often have a way of creating a dynamic environment and helping people work toward challenging goals.

Strengths of Pioneering Leaders
- They tend to be good at initiating change.
- They often trust their gut instincts.
- They're able to bring people together to achieve their goals.
- They tend to be inspiring.
- They're not afraid to try something new.
- They're comfortable taking the lead.
- They set stretch goals for themselves and others.
- They aren't afraid to take risks.

Through years of leader-watching and research, we've developed three essential lessons that Pioneering leaders have to offer. These three lessons are built around Pioneering leaders' tendencies to climb and expand. If you think of yourself as a Pioneering leader, these lessons should validate your primary leadership dimension. Or, if you feel that your leadership could use a boost from the Pioneering Dimension, use these three lessons and their complementary suggestions to channel your inner pioneer.

Three Essential Lessons from Pioneering Leaders
- The next big thing isn't hiding under your desk
- A leader's job is change
- Overplanning can be as dangerous as underplanning

In this chapter, we'll explore these three lessons, dig into the obstacles that not-so-Pioneering leaders might face, and offer suggestions for how to bring these lessons to life. Not all of the observations here will describe any one leader perfectly, but we think you'll gain some very useful insights into your fundamental assumptions and thought patterns around being Pioneering.

Lesson One: The Next Big Thing Isn't Hiding under Your Desk

Pioneering leaders know that innovation doesn't happen without exploration. The world is not only complex, but it's also constantly changing. As a leader, it's important to understand the context in which you lead. Often, the leader's world is governed by external factors, and Pioneering leaders are good at keeping up with shifting demands. Leaders who are low on the Pioneering Dimension—often those whose styles fall on the southern side of the model—take great pride in their own logic, and as a result, they may often stay on a path that makes sense on paper, even when it doesn't align with more dynamic variables. The danger in this, of course, is becoming a team or an organization that isn't in touch with the demands of the fast-moving world.

Big Suggestion One: Actively Seek New Opportunities beyond Your Organization's Walls

Pioneering leaders recognize that the world rarely acts the way it *should,* and leaders need to be responsive to the way the world actually *is.* Therefore, they allow themselves to think outside of how things have always been done and to explore the cutting-edge improvements being made in the field. Unfortunately, many not-so-Pioneering leaders have very narrowly defined views of how things *should* work—how things *should* go. And, when these leaders build their beliefs on logic that they see as impeccable, it's tough for them to see when their beliefs are actually a few degrees off from reality. At times, they may construct a plan in a vacuum, and from their limited perspective, the plan *seems* to be a real thing of beauty. When things don't end up working as they thought they would, they may find themselves saying, "Well, they *would* work if people just did things the way they *should* do them," or thinking, "This would work if the business world acted the way it should."

Is It Worth It?

There are many benefits in taking the Pioneering leader's approach and being more responsive to the dynamic world. Simply put, results matter. Intentions are great, and planning is important, but in the end, things need to work. Demands need to be met, often on a tight schedule. This is the way the world works today. In order to do this well, leaders need to respond to internal and external data—whether that be customer feedback, sales figures, or changing technologies. Leaders must take this information and quickly adapt their assumptions to find new opportunities that meet the current situation. Many leaders whose styles fall on the southern side of the model report that they wish they'd learned this earlier in their careers—things like, "make the most of opportunities," "research opportunities," "don't pass on opportunities," "be aggressive about exploring opportunities," "always be on the lookout for opportunities," and "take advantage of opportunities." See a theme here?

By learning to adapt more quickly to new information, you can help to create a more nimble organization. This can help you take advantage of important opportunities that require timeliness. Sure, it's sometimes difficult to change course when you firmly believe that your original plan is the better way, but when you're getting feedback that something else is called for, you need to listen. Persistence can be a double-edged sword, and in this case, too much of it can hurt you. Yes, it's important to keep working hard toward reaching your goals, but that doesn't mean stubbornly latching on to an idea whose day has passed.

Potential Obstacles to Actively Seeking New Opportunities for Not-So-Pioneering Leaders

- You may not always think that change is called for.
- You may prefer to take a clear path toward a goal, leaving little room for random variables and opportunities.
- You may be caught up in how things ought to be or used to be.
- You may be so caught up in solving problems that you get tunnel vision and fail to look beyond the current task.
- You may get so caught up in the details that you don't consider the big picture.
- You may be so comfortable with your current vision that new opportunities seem risky.

Taking Action

Focus on three ideas when it comes to actively seeking new opportunities beyond your organization's walls: invite, follow, and reflect. First, **invite** the people you work with to share their perspectives on new directions that the group could or should pursue. Let them know what you're thinking, and welcome their suggestions, even if their ideas compete with your own. Next, **follow** thought leaders in your industry and stay on top of best practices. Things are constantly changing, and it's not enough to rely on your training and experience. You need to be a student of your field. If this is something you don't have a lot of time for, recruit people to help you. Have lunch regularly with people who read journals, go to tradeshows, and who simply know a lot of people. Finally, when you get strong pushback on how things are currently being done, **reflect** on what you are hearing. This is particularly true if the information is coming from people who are working in the trenches or interacting with customers more often than you are. Be ready to recognize new opportunities right under your nose.

Lesson Two: A Leader's Job is Change

Pioneering leaders know that a leader's job is change, and they aren't afraid to stretch the boundaries of what's been done before. Many leaders who are lower on the Pioneering Dimension, on the other hand, strive to create a world of peace and stability, and this is, in many ways, in conflict with change. Harmony is a major priority for many leaders, and this is true in terms of relationships, tasks, and environments. Situations that might feel stagnant to Pioneering leaders may feel comfortable to those leaders who view predictability as a good thing. In fact, many leaders whose styles fall on the southern side of the model build structures and routines that help them avoid chaos or surprises altogether. Obviously, leaders must strike a balance, but the very nature of leadership is to take people—or an organization—from here to there, and that requires change.

Big Suggestion Two: Break Some Glass

Imagine, for a moment, what it would feel like to literally smash a pane of glass with a hammer. We're not asking you to do this literally—though we know one leader who actually had people do this as an exercise—but we're asking you to stray from your comfort zone. This is particularly true if you're the type of leader who likes getting up each morning knowing what to expect. Our research shows that stretching the boundaries of what's possible is an often-requested leadership behavior for leaders who are low on the Pioneering Dimension. In fact, this behavior is highly requested of all leaders, but it tends to feel least natural for those whose styles fall on the southern side of the model. When leaders take their aversion to change to the extreme, the result can be personal and organizational mediocrity. If we always trust our guts to tell us when to take a risk and never push beyond our comfort zones, we will probably miss out on some great, relatively safe opportunities. When it comes to taking chances, research shows that people often overstate the risks involved and under-emphasize the potential rewards (Kahneman & Tversky, 1979).

Is It Worth It?

First, it may be helpful to consider what, exactly, sets leaders apart from others, We believe that, among other things, leaders are called to *lead change,* not simply to maintain what's always been done. Sure, leaders need to create a sense of stability for those around them, but they also need to ensure the future vitality of the organization by avoiding stagnation. An effective leader should encourage growth—both for individuals and the organization—not to mention for themselves! In our study, we had a number of leaders who wished they had more often "pushed the envelope" earlier in their careers.

What happens when leaders don't take some chances, break some glass, or push the envelope? One danger is becoming increasingly out of touch with current thought leadership and best practices. When leaders like to stick with what's comfortable, they don't entertain adventurous ideas that could lead to huge payoffs for the organization. Also, if the leader isn't willing to consider innovative ideas, people will feel discouraged from taking chances. As you can imagine, this would be incredibly frustrating for many people—especially those who are particularly driven. No leader wants to quash the creativity and entrepreneurial spirit of their organization. By learning to break some glass, you'll help to ensure the future health of your organization.

Potential Obstacles To Breaking Some Glass for Not-So-Pioneering Leaders

- You may work hard to create a stable environment.
- You may not see your job as deliberately taking people into situations with a high potential for misfire.

- You may inflict a lot of pressure on yourself to get things right.
- You may consume too much energy with uncertainty about your decisions.
- You may simply be more comfortable running things according to current methods.

Taking Action

Consider three ideas when it comes to breaking some glass: trust, act, and push. First, **trust** your own ideas and challenge yourself to offer your opinion before you have absolute certainty. Many not-so-Pioneering leaders spend a great deal of time ruminating over their thoughts for fear of taking a misstep. By doing this, you may be missing out on opportunities to share some of your best ideas. Second, look at breaking some glass as the chance to **act** on your beliefs. As a leader, you can have tremendous influence, but your vision can't be acted upon if your voice isn't heard. Finally, remember to **push** ahead. It's tempting to keep on doing what you know, but if you're intentional about moving forward, you'll bring up the energy level of those around you. Give yourself permission to take some chances, and remember that *not* taking any chances presents its own dangers.

Lesson Three: Over-planning Can Be as Dangerous as Under-planning

Managers make sure that plans are executed, but Pioneering leaders take things a step further—they promote bold action and take the group into new territory. This requires being out in front and moving at a fast pace. Leaders who are low on the Pioneering Dimension have some characteristics that make it difficult to take bold action. Security and stability are high priorities for these leaders, many of whom have primary dimensions on the southern side of the model. Compared to Pioneering leaders, they're more likely to tolerate a lack of variety, and they may often choose to perform tasks that are a little dull rather than throwing themselves into chaotic situations. Detailed planning helps them create safe settings free of doubt, anxiety, and unpleasant interpersonal exchanges. Pioneering leaders, on the other hand, know that leaders must sometimes take chances. What can the rest of us learn from these daring and adventurous leaders?

Big Suggestion Three: Learn to Take Leaps of Faith

Because many leaders can often get so caught up in over-planning that they miss out on important opportunities, we'd like to see you learn to take leaps of faith. Not only *take* leaps of faith, but create an environment where others feel empowered to do the same. If you're naturally a risk-averse person, this won't feel natural to you, but we think you'll find ways to adopt this suggestion while remaining true to your personal leadership approach. We're not asking that you stop doing your homework entirely. We're simply suggesting that you learn to take decisive action after allowing for a reasonable amount of analysis.

Is It Worth It?

Let's explore the benefits of taking leaps of faith. It's probably not news to you that most innovations stem from trying something that is initially unproven. In order to hit on a breakthrough, you must be willing to lower your threshold for how much certainty is needed. If you're low on the Pioneering Dimension, your current threshold may be too high. Sure, careful planning reduces the possibility of failure, but it also reduces the possibility of real growth. In order to learn to take leaps of faith more often, you must be more open to the occasional failure. Once in a while, you will let other people down, and that may be hard for you to swallow.

However, there are many benefits to taking this risk. Keep in mind that the consequences of your decisions are often less than what you imagine them to be. Many leaders have overactive imaginations in this sense. The potential consequences of your action may be less troublesome than the potential consequences of your inaction. When leaders are indecisive or stick with the status quo too often, many people become disengaged. People whose approaches fall on the northern side of the model tend to be adventurous and crave variety. As a leader, if you build an entirely stable environment, many of those people are likely to tune out—it's simply not stimulating for them. Not only that, but if you aren't able to keep up with what's current in your industry, the entire organization may miss out on potentially beneficial opportunities. As a leader, there will be times when you lead people down the wrong path, but your job is still to forge ahead.

Potential Obstacles to Taking Leaps of Faith For Not-So-Pioneering Leaders

- You may be uncomfortable acting without understanding the exact nature of the risk.
- You may be afraid to let go of control.
- You may not like to make decisions based on limited information.
- You may have trouble taking the nimble posture necessary to adjust to changing circumstances.
- You may resist putting more weight on forward momentum and less on perfectionism.
- You may need to become more comfortable with urgency.

Taking Action

Focus on three ideas when it comes to learning to take leaps of faith: entertain, start, and limit. First, allow yourself to **entertain** adventurous ideas that may initially scare you. Try to think more about what could work than what could go wrong. This is especially true when others bring ideas to you. Give them a chance to tell you about the potential benefits. Remember, there's no risk in entertaining. Next, **start** taking small leaps of faith. Try not to look at being more adventurous as a scary, life-changing goal. Look for little opportunities here and there for small leaps of faith. Sure, even small changes may disrupt stability, but focus on the long-term benefits, which may even include *increased* stability. Finally, **limit** the amount of time that you allow yourself to analyze new opportunities. Don't let yourself get caught up in "analysis paralysis." You can absolutely weigh the potential costs and benefits, but there's often a point of diminishing returns. Don't allow yourself to miss a great opportunity just because you're afraid to commit. If you've done your homework, give yourself permission to take a leap of faith.

Conclusion

Whatever your primary leadership dimension, it's valuable to adopt some of the Pioneering leader's adventurous, charismatic, inspiring, and daring ways, even if ever so slightly. Specifically, to be more Pioneering:

- Actively seek new opportunities beyond your organization's walls,
- Break some glass, and
- Learn to take leaps of faith.

Case Study: Break Some Glass.

We talked to Genevra, a senior product manager at a manufacturing and consumer goods company, about how she's learned to break some glass. She's had a great role model in terms of learning to not be afraid to shake things up. "I have a really, really great boss and she was brought into the company to do that—to change everything—and it has been working extremely well, and she has been pushing the envelope on a lot of things." Genevra is an Inclusive leader, so breaking glass doesn't come naturally to her, though she welcomed the dynamic approach of her new boss. "I thought it was exciting just because I was ready for it," she said, "but yeah, for some other people, it kind of freaked them out a little bit. But they're seeing now that it works. It's been very good." We asked Genevra what advice she would give her younger self. "Mainly I would say, just speak your opinion. Don't be so afraid to step behind and be aggressive about what you believe in. Like if you believe you know something is supposed to be this way, don't be shy and hold it back if you're afraid someone might think it's a bad idea." There may be a variety of barriers that leaders face when it comes to breaking glass—risk aversion, a lack of confidence in their ideas, or fear of upsetting others— but many leaders like Genevra learn that change can be exactly what an organization needs.

Chapter 12

Lessons from Energizing Leaders

What Can We Learn from Energizing Leaders?

Energizing leaders help organizations focus on building a dynamic, engaging atmosphere. Their instinct is to humanize and bring emotional connection to their work. In this era of service-based work, the organization's most important assets walk out the door each day and go home to their families and friends. As we discussed in Chapter 2, the Energizing Dimension is located in the northeastern area of the 8 Dimensions of Leadership Model, which means that they tend to be fast-paced and outspoken, as well as warm and accepting. The Energizing leader maintains a focus on the people side of the business and has much to teach leaders who may focus more on processes, analyses, operations, and strategies.

Energizing leaders want to collaborate with others, to explore adventurous ideas, and more than anything, to show and build enthusiasm. They tend to be extremely gregarious. Not only do they energize social settings, but they're skilled at building and maintaining professional networks. Leaders who are high on the Energizing Dimension often have so much energy that they have trouble sitting still. They're eager to maintain their momentum, and they tend to get bored easily. Frankly, it takes a lot of energy to be an Energizing leader, but they come by it naturally. They have a seemingly unlimited supply of optimism, and they do their best to bring up the spirits of those around them.

There's a great deal to celebrate about leaders who primarily use the Energizing Dimension. Their leadership legitimacy comes from their sincere passion. It's clear that Energizing leaders honestly believe in what they're selling—even if the "products" are just ideas—and this makes people more inclined to follow. People are generally attracted to leaders who seem to be 100% invested in their visions and in their organizations' missions. Energizing leaders often have a talent for bringing people together to work on mutual goals. They have an openness about them that allows them to share their opinions and feelings quite freely, and, because they tend to be adventurous, they welcome change.

Strengths of Energizing Leaders

- They're able to rally people around group goals.
- They tend to look on the bright side.
- They're comfortable being in the spotlight.
- They're often accepting of other people's ideas.
- They take the time to celebrate accomplishments.
- They build solid professional networks.
- They have a knack for selling ideas.
- They show appreciation for other people's contributions.

As you can see, Energizing leaders bring many assets to the table. As one high-energy leader put it, "I really try and more inspire people and kind of just give them the tools to succeed—to be more of an orchestra leader in the organization, helping people do the best in their own jobs." Energizing leaders have a fundamental belief in the power of optimism: they believe it motivates everyone to work harder, including themselves.

Organizations rely on these leaders to bring passion and conviction to the work. These leaders demand that their teams or organizations celebrate the small successes toward the larger goals. People rely on Energizing leaders for their understanding and contribution to making their environments great places to work. Below are three important lessons built around Energizing leaders' tendencies to keep things positive, build connections, and focus on people. If Energizing is your primary leadership dimension, these lessons should validate your personal style. Or, if you feel that your leadership could be a little more Energizing, use these three lessons and their complementary suggestions to strengthen this dimension.

Three Essential Lessons from Energizing Leaders
- People need enthusiasm to reach their goals.
- Sometimes it does matter who you know.
- Emotions are the connective tissue of the team.

In this chapter, we'll explore these three lessons, dig into the obstacles that not-so-Energizing leaders might face, and offer suggestions for how to bring these lessons to life. Not all of the observations here will describe any one leader perfectly, but we think you'll gain some very useful insights into your fundamental assumptions and thought patterns around being Energizing.

Lesson One: People Need Enthusiasm to Reach Their Goals

Energizing leaders have a transparent way of showing their passion and enthusiasm for the group's goals. Many people need to feel excited about goals and to feel that their contributions are recognized. Leaders who are low on the Energizing Dimension may rely on other things such as drive, conviction, and the challenge of overcoming obstacles to reach their goals. Some leaders are even skeptical of the emotional appeals characteristic of Energizing leaders, and they may have difficulty generating enthusiasm and doling out praise. Leaders who are low on the

Energizing Dimension don't tend to give rah-rah speeches and want to keep things logical and professional. In their minds, their job as a leader is to take a more hard-nosed, down-to-business approach. Energizing leaders use a more positive approach to get people excited about performing.

Big Suggestion One: Make an Effort to Build Enthusiasm for the Group's Goals

Energizing leaders don't necessarily need to be intentional about building enthusiasm—it comes naturally to them. However, you may need to be more purposeful in your efforts. As a leader, it's critical that you understand that people are motivated by a variety of factors, all of which are valid. Picture the 8 Dimensions of Leadership Model. If your approach is, say Deliberate, you're motivated to solve problems, expand your expertise, and turn out high quality work. Consider the opposite side of the model. Leaders with the Energizing approach need to have a sense of optimism, camaraderie with the people they'll be working with, and a positive environment. That's just one example. The point is that some people require enthusiasm from you as a leader before you'll gain their alignment.

Is It Worth It?

Let's start with a small study on the impact of a leader's mood on the team (Sy et al., 2005). Researchers separated the leaders of small groups into two conditions. Leaders in the "positive mood" condition saw a humorous eight-minute video clip (i.e., David Letterman) and leaders in the "negative mood" condition saw a somber eight-minute clip (i.e., a documentary on social injustice and aggression). The leaders then went about leading their groups on a task. After just seven minutes of interaction, followers of positive mood leaders showed significantly better moods. That is, it took very little time for the leader's mood to spread to the rest of the group. What's more interesting, however, is that those groups also showed much better coordination of their activities. There was greater efficiency and less wasted effort. Presumably, when people are in a better mood, they are more agreeable and communication is much smoother. The point is, all of these positive benefits were due to the leaders' moods, and they might not even have been aware of it. Imagine what's possible when a leader deliberately sets out to build enthusiasm. This is especially true when the team faces an impasse.

Now, when things get tough, people handle it in a variety of ways. Some people become more determined, while others are more easily distracted or discouraged by obstacles. Simply having a goal may be enough for particularly driven people, but it's not always enough for others. By building enthusiasm for shared goals, you help people see that they're part of something bigger than themselves. You make them feel needed, and you help them to see how their everyday actions play into the big picture. Many people perform better when others are counting on them, and as a leader, you can help them see how everyone's contributions are related. Most importantly, you can help people to feel emotionally invested in the goal. They'll understand its importance, and they'll care whether the group is able to execute the vision as planned.

Leaders who are not as comfortable with the Energizing Dimension can have a tendency to be emotionally detached from others, particularly in a professional setting. Why is this problematic? Because as a leader, having people attach themselves to you and your vision is how you gain alignment. This means sending out signals that make people actually *want* to attach to you—not out of fear, but out of respect and inspiration. This requires a more open approach than some leaders may be initially comfortable with, but if you're able to show more emotion— simply to show the real you—you will invite people to connect with you in a more meaningful way. Not only that, but they'll more readily get on board with your vision. To the extent that you remain private and guarded, people will keep their distance.

Potential Obstacles to Making an Effort to Build Enthusiasm
for the Group's Goals for Not-So-Energizing Leaders

- You may see conjuring up a well of positive emotions as beneath you.
- You may struggle to let your emotions flow freely.
- You may feel that showing unbridled positive emotion is entirely out of the question! (You may resent that we just used an exclamation mark.)
- You may be more comfortable maintaining your game face, even if it means holding your hopes and dreams inside.
- You may have an unconscious instinct to "keep people in their place."
- You may have a tendency to keep people's expectations of the future in check.

Taking Action

Consider three ideas when it comes to making an effort to build enthusiasm for the group's goals: brainstorm, hold, and build. First, **brainstorm** a variety of ways you could build enthusiasm in your group or organization. What has worked well in the past? What do other leaders do to build enthusiasm? Borrow ideas from those who are good at generating energy. Next, **hold** regular meetings to ensure that people are kept up to speed with projects and initiatives. Help them to see how their efforts fit into the big-picture goals of the group or organization. Paint a picture of where you're headed. Even if you don't have the gift of gab, find your own way of telling a story about your goals. People connect with stories, and research suggests that they specifically find metaphors to be inspiring (Mio et al, 2005). Also remember that even if you find it easier to focus on challenges, be sure to highlight what's been going well. By communicating regularly about team goals, you can create better alignment around your vision. Finally, **build** enthusiasm by being intentional about building your team. Make time for teambuilding events and informal opportunities to socialize. Get outside of your day-to-day routines and learn something about each other and how you work as a team. Don't just show people your enthusiasm for specific projects—show them what gets you excited about life.

Lesson Two: Sometimes It Does Matter Who You Know

Energizing leaders are gregarious people who naturally build and maintain large personal and professional networks, and this can be a real asset to their leadership capabilities. Leaders who are more private may dislike, possibly even abhor, the idea of setting out to make new connections, but this really is an essential piece of the leadership puzzle. Happily, today's technology offers a wide variety of new networking opportunities that may appeal to leaders who are less comfortable with the Energizing Dimension. Regardless of the methods you use to build your network, you never know when the right contact will be able to help you pursue new opportunities for your organization, help you hire the right people, or give you just the perspective you need to make a big decision.

Big Suggestion Two: Be Intentional about Making Connections with a Wide Variety of People

Because they're so people-oriented, Energizing leaders don't have to think twice about making connections with a wide variety of people. They're not only interested in hearing people's stories, but they like to tell their own, and they're quick to make friends wherever they go. These leaders are "connectors" who love to introduce like-minded folks who might be able to help each other. And naturally, they welcome such introductions from others. If you are not an outgoing person by nature, this suggestion will seem far less fun. In fact, it will make work out of something that others consider to be the highest form of entertainment. Undoubtedly, there is some skill involved in networking, and you may have noticed the increased prevalence of "speed networking" events that are offered as professional development in higher education communities and professional associations.

Is It Worth It?

When leaders stick to the same routine day after day and fail to make connections outside of the organization's walls, they miss out on opportunities not just for themselves, but for their organizations. We're not just talking about schmoozing with lots of people so you'll have a leg up on your next job search. We're talking about having collegial relationships with peers in your industry—or even in entirely different industries—with whom you can bounce ideas around and call on for advice during unique situations. For example, as we developed the leadership model for this book and other related products, we called on a wide range of friends and acquaintances who know a thing or two about leadership. We were able to test our theories against their expertise, gain some outside perspective, and get referrals to other subject matter experts.

Networking is also just as important within your organization. One recent empirical study concluded that leaders' effectiveness at change implementation was only measurable when the leaders' efforts were considered in aggregate (O'Reilly et al., 2010). That is, the lone leader did not make a perceptible impact, but when leaders were aligned across different levels, change began to happen. Without strong, fluid relationships within your organization, you will have difficulty initiating this type of alignment.

One Commanding leader in the IT field told us, "I should have done a better job of networking and meeting with more people to learn from and identify opportunities." It's not just the shy leaders who fail to build solid professional networks— sometimes the most driven leaders simply don't make the time to reach out. Other leaders in our research noted that they wish they'd been better about following up after networking opportunities. How many times have you met someone who would be a great contact but failed to do anything to extend the relationship beyond the chance meeting at a conference or social function? What opportunities might you have missed out on? You'll never know, but by being more intentional about this in the future, you'll set yourself up to have a more solid network to participate in, both by adding value and asking for help.

Potential Obstacles to Making Connections with a Wide Variety of People for Not-So-Energizing Leaders

- You may not take the time to network.
- You may have anxiety about interacting socially with new people.
- You may see little value in networking.
- You may feel that you don't have enough opportunities to make new connections.
- You may feel that networking isn't as relevant in your field.
- You may be unsure how to find the type of people with whom you'd like to connect..

Taking Action

Focus on three ideas when it comes to making connections with a wide variety of people: reconnect, participate, and leave. First, make an effort to **reconnect** with any key contacts that you haven't talked to in a while. Send a friendly note, invite someone to lunch, or simply pick up the phone to touch base. Find out what they're working on and what's going on for them personally. Next, **participate** in professional networking online. This is an outstanding tool for those who are less social by nature. Join the major social networking sites and if it's of interest to you, try blogging or microblogging. These are all good ways to connect and keep track of what people are working on, reading, and thinking. Finally, **leave** the comfort of your office. You're not going to make new connections if you never widen your circle. Remind yourself of the benefit of attending conferences, benefits, and alumni association events. All of these settings offer rewards beyond the social, as well. Then, when you meet people out and about, take the step to cement your connection by following up. Take the stack of business cards that you collect at a conference and reach out to those people once you're back at home. If you told someone that you'd send them some information, do it. Making connections takes some effort, but the potential returns are great.

Lesson Three: Emotions Are the Connective Tissue of the Team

Leadership is more than just managing programs. Leaders are also responsible for unifying the group and leading the rally. The cognitive part of this is aligning people around a specific goal. But there is an emotional part, too, and though it may not be every leader's cup of tea, team spirit does matter. Some leaders have tendencies that can make the emotional aspects of leadership more difficult. In fact, tending to the emotional side of the organization may feel like a distraction from what these types see as their *real* responsibilities.

Big Suggestion Three: Learn to Lead the Rally

As a leader, you're in a unique position to help create a sense of community—a feeling that people are in it together, that the whole is greater than the sum of the parts. To achieve truly outstanding outcomes, it's not enough to be a group of loosely connected people working toward a common goal. Great collaboration happens when people learn to rely on each other and are willing to extend themselves to help each other. We'd like to see you learn how to lead the rally by providing inspiration for others and keeping them fully engaged.

Is It Worth It?

Let's explore the benefits of learning to lead the rally. Simply put, people want to see your passion for the work you're doing. Not only that, but they want to know that you believe in them and their ability to achieve their goals. Sure, they may see someone who is trustworthy and fair, but this only inspires a certain level of commitment. When a leader doesn't bring an emotional element to the work, the organization or team may feel a little cold, particularly to those whose approaches fall on the eastern side of the model.

Our research shows that people are looking for more emotional investment from Resolute, Deliberate, and Humble leaders. For example "rallying people to achieve goals" was requested by fifty percent of the people who rated Deliberate leaders. This tells us that if you can learn to lead the rally more effectively, you have a great chance of improving your overall leadership performance. Dealing with feelings may seem like a waste of time compared to other leadership roles you fill, but it's both entirely worth your time and within your reach.

Potential Obstacles to Learning to Lead the Rally for Not-So-Energizing Leaders

- You may have a tendency to be more autonomous than team-oriented.
- You may see your job as simply making decisions, providing resources, and showing accountability.
- You may not see the need for a lot of praise, compliments, or encouragement.
- You may want to avoid coming across as phony or insincere.
- You may see dealing with emotions as an obstacle to getting the job done.
- You may not see yourself as particularly inspirational.

Taking Action

Consider three ideas when it comes to learning to lead the rally: ask, generate, and engage. First, **ask** people what they find most motivating. Learn what makes people with other styles tick. You can start by reading some of the other chapters in this book and spending time with people in your organization. If you can connect group goals to people's personal interests and aspirations, they're likely to be more engaged. Next, **generate** interest in group goals by explaining how people's contributions will fit into the big picture. Explain what's in it for them, as well as what's in it for the organization. Tell them exactly why this piece—their piece—of the puzzle matters. Build them up so they feel a sense of purpose. Your goal is to get them emotionally invested in the vision, and a key factor in this is showing that you are emotionally invested first. If people don't seem engaged, name the feelings that you see and start a conversation. For example, "It seems like the team is a little discouraged or disengaged lately." Finally, **engage** people by practicing the art of working as a team. That's right—it might take practice! One fun way to show people that teamwork matters to you is to organize an event that benefits a charity. Take a break to have your whole team volunteer together. The possibilities are endless, but people might enjoy building something, walking in a 5K, or serving food at a shelter. Practice inspiring people to achieve group goals in a unique setting like this, and then spend some time thinking about how to lead the rally more effectively in your daily leadership practice.

Conclusion

No matter your primary leadership dimension, it's valuable to adopt some of the Energizing leader's lively, outgoing, and enthusiastic ways, even if ever so slightly. Specifically, to be more Energizing:

- Make an effort to build enthusiasm for the group's goals,

- Be intentional about making connections with a wide variety of people, and
- Learn to lead the rally.

Case Study: Be Intentional About Making Connections with a Wide Variety of People

Carla is an experienced IT executive at a large insurance company. We talked to her about lessons she wished she'd learned at the outset of her leadership career, and she mentioned that she had trouble seeing the big picture. More importantly, she struggled to put what she was doing into a larger context or to explain her vision to a broader audience, mostly because she simply didn't know people, and they didn't know her. "I guess I would have spent more time making relationships outside of my specific area of responsibility," she said, "so that I had a better understanding of what the bigger picture was." She added that such relationships would have provided the support she needed when she wanted to move things forward, and they also might have given her better insight into what others needed from her. "I think that I would have moved more quickly [in my career] if I had a broader group of support," she said. "I don't think people knew me." As she's developed as a leader, Carla has gained the confidence to reach out to others, especially as she's seen firsthand the value in doing so. She told us a story about someone who resigned because she didn't feel appreciated and didn't see much opportunity for herself. Carla noted that to get into the leadership ranks, it's often not enough just to do good work. "You have to sell yourself," she said. "You have to be known. People aren't going to come to you to see if you have value. You have to demonstrate it to them. You have to be more outgoing." For leaders like her who aren't naturally inclined to reach out, Carla recommended starting to build their networks slowly. "Start establishing small relationships outside of your work," she said, "and then move bigger."

Chapter 13

Lessons from Affirming Leaders

What Can We Learn from Affirming Leaders?

Whether you consider yourself high or low on the Affirming Dimension, we'll help you understand the benefits of this positive approach. As we discussed in Chapter 2, the Affirming Dimension is located on the eastern side of the 8 Dimensions of Leadership Model, which means that Affirming leaders tend to be exceptionally warm and accepting. We'll explore some key characteristics that make up the Affirming Dimension of leadership.

Affirming leaders want to encourage groups to succeed, to engage others in open communication, and more than anything, to create a positive, collaborative environment. They tend to maintain informal relationships with the people they lead, and one of their gifts as leaders is to create a sense of cohesion. People feel personally connected to the leader and connected to each other, and this helps members of the group to perceive themselves as a team rather than a group of individuals working toward the same goal. Affirming leaders generally aren't as geared toward independence as some other leaders. This is positive in that they look for opportunities to collaborate, and in some regards, they can seem almost egoless. They take almost as much pride in seeing someone else come up with a brilliant idea as in coming up with it themselves. They take joy in building on that idea and connecting with the other person.

There are many benefits to the Affirming approach. Affirming leaders have a genuine interest in listening to others, and they're also willing to share. Their communication is often a very balanced give and take, and people who interact with them often feel understood and accepted immediately. This is the heart of their leadership effectiveness, and people have the sense that Affirming leaders care for them and will be their advocate. These leaders have a laid-back approach, and many people see them as approachable and considerate. All of their relationship-oriented strengths make Affirming leaders well suited to lead collaborative efforts and bring people together around shared goals.

Strengths of Affirming Leaders

- They tend to be friendly and approachable.
- They're often generous in their praise.
- They're able to consider the needs of different groups of people.
- They're less concerned with their own ego needs.
- They tend to be optimistic.
- They're good at making people feel that they belong.
- They're able to see things from other perspectives.
- They often come across as down-to-earth.

As you can see, Affirming leaders have many important strengths to offer to their organizations and to the world. Based on these strengths, we've developed three key lessons that they bring. These lessons are all related to Affirming leaders' tendencies to be people-oriented and patient. If you consider yourself an Affirming leader, these lessons should resonate with how you currently lead. Or perhaps you feel like your leadership could stand a little more from the Affirming Dimension, and in that case, these three lessons are a great place to start.

Three Essential Lessons from Affirming Leaders

- Crossing the finish line won't do much good if your team is in shreds when it gets there.
- People come to work for more than just a paycheck.
- People aren't going to act the way you think they should.

In this chapter, we'll explore these three lessons, touch on the obstacles that not-so-Affirming leaders might face, and offer suggestions for how to bring these lessons to life. Not all of the observations here will describe any one leader perfectly, but we think you'll gain some very useful insights into your fundamental assumptions and thought patterns around being Affirming.

Lesson One: Crossing the Finish Line Won't Do Much Good If Your Team Is in Shreds When It Gets There

We're the first to admit that results matter. Quality matters. But do leaders also have responsibility for the emotional well-being of the people they lead? Consider a recent study (Gaddis et al., 2004) in which participants were asked to work on a project, after which they would be given feedback by a group leader. All of them were told that they had failed the task and would need to try again. Here's the catch: some of the participants got feedback from a leader who was positive. The leader was upbeat and relaxed and expressed gratitude to the participants. Other participants got feedback from a leader who was negative. The leader was irritated, sighed heavily, folded arms across the chest, and gave a forced "thank you." As you would expect, the positive leaders were rated as much more effective. But what about the participants' performances? Did the negative leaders push them to do better? Actually, the opposite happened. Participants who had a positive leader had significantly better performances. Further, participants who had a negative leader actually performed more poorly on their second attempts. When leaders don't pay attention to emotional variables, quality and results suffer.

Ultimately, leaders are responsible for creating a sense of community where people can feel good about their contributions. Affirming leaders are great at building teams. When things go well, they make a point to recognize people whose efforts made a difference, and when things fall apart, they're willing to share in the blame. Affirming leaders tend to create friendly environments where everyone feels like a valuable member of the group, individual needs are taken into account, and people feel like their input is valued.

Big Suggestion One: Monitor Your "Default" Expressions

Affirming leaders make people feel comfortable with friendly expressions that send a positive message. Leaders who are lower on the Affirming Dimension may not do this as naturally or as readily. Now, we're not saying that you need to be everyone's best friend. What we're suggesting is that you learn to monitor the "default" expressions you use that may intimidate or demoralize others. We have some personal experience with this. In college, one of us learned that others often found her intimidating, simply because she didn't walk around campus with a big grin on her face. She dubbed this her "bad default face," and it stuck! Over the years, she has learned to monitor her expressions, and this has helped her to network and to be seen as more approachable. Many leaders are simply so absorbed in thought that they don't realize how they come across to others. They may put forth a stern front when this isn't their intention at all.

Is It Worth It?

What's the risk of coming across as intimidating as a leader? When you give off negative vibes and say things with a harsh tone, people may not feel personally invested in being part of your team. Sure, you might reach your performance goals as a group for a time, but it may not be sustainable in the long run. If people have strong negative associations with the group's work, they're going to burn out. Where will that get you? High turnover rates, lack of engagement, and bitterness. People will invest in their work on a surface level, but they simply won't pour their hearts into it.

If you can adjust your behavior to come across as less intimidating—warm, even—you'll experience many improvements in your relationships with others. First, you'll seem more approachable. You'll come across as a leader who has empathy for others, and this can lead to increased trust between you and the members of your group. This in turn allows others to be themselves. If you want to get the best out of people, there are more productive means of motivation than fear. How about empowerment with a side of accountability?

Potential Obstacles to Monitoring "Default" Expressions for Not-So-Affirming Leaders

- You may resent the fact that you even need to censor your moods.

- You may think that other people should just toughen up a little.

- You may think that there's nothing wrong with being candid.

- You may not believe in sugarcoating the truth.

- You may have grown attached to the power that comes with being intimidating.

Taking Action

If you're less comfortable with the Affirming Dimension, consider three ideas when it comes to being more aware of your "default" expressions: focus, initiate, and assume. First, **focus** specifically on being friendly. This means greeting people when they approach you, making eye contact, and using positive body language and gestures. When you need to give feedback, be conscientious about your tone and the constructiveness of your criticism. Next, make an effort to **initiate** more lighthearted conversations. This can go a long way to breaking down barriers between you and others. Be proactive about asking questions and getting to know people. Allow yourself to have fun and show your less serious side. All too often, leaders who are low on the Affirming Dimension are so focused on solving problems that they neglect the relationship side of leadership. Finally, work to **assume** good intentions when working with other people. As we've discussed, many leaders can be quick to show their disgust. Try operating under the assumption that people are genuinely making their best effort. It's easy to forget that people often approach tasks differently than we would. By assuming the best in others, you may be less quick to show a scowl or a let out a disapproving sigh.

Lesson Two: People Come to Work for More Than Just a Paycheck

Affirming leaders know that there's an emotional component to being part of a group, and they try to make everyone feel valued. Leaders who find the Affirming Dimension less natural may overlook this important aspect of leadership, for a variety of reasons. Some may be too demanding, others in too much of a hurry, and still others simply too low-key to be very demonstrative of their appreciation. Or, they may have so much confidence in their own ideas that they don't even really *see* the value of what other people bring to the table—let alone thank them for it. Affirming leaders don't have high ego needs, and they're genuinely interested in collaboration, so they tend to be generous with their praise and slow to criticize.

Big Suggestion Two: Let People Know That You Value Them

When leaders consistently neglect to acknowledge contributions over time, people start to feel that they don't really matter. After a while, their motivation is likely to lag—especially if they have a high need for praise and recognition. If you've been leading for a while, you know that people have vastly different needs in this area. Some are happy with a quiet thank you or a bonus check, while others find public recognition more gratifying. And that's just on a personal level—what about recognizing teams of people or even the whole organization? The point of letting people know that you value them is not only to make them feel good, but also to help you start to notice more often the efforts, big and small, that are taking place right under your nose.

Is It Worth It?

Let's explore the benefits of letting people know that you value them. As a starting point, consider why *you* go to work each day. Is it just for the paycheck? Chances are good that it's not. Regardless of your leadership style, part of the reason that you show up is probably to reap the rewards of having your efforts recognized. Would a personal victory be gratifying if no one knew that it happened? Maybe. But it would probably be a lot more fun if you had some supporters patting you on the back and letting you know that what you did was really something. It's really that simple. People want to be part of something bigger than themselves, and as a leader, you can affirm that they are.

What happens when Affirming leaders acknowledge people's contributions? Generally speaking, those people want to keep doing good things. It's simple positive reinforcement. Not only that, but when you go out of your way to let someone know that you appreciate their efforts, they'll start to value you more as a leader. They'll grow to respect you, to trust you, and to want to keep doing great work for you. As a leader, you can create a culture where people feel valued, or you can create a culture where people don't see why they really matter. Seems like an easy answer, right?

Potential Obstacles to Letting People Know That You Value
Them For Not-So-Affirming Leaders

- You may be so fast-paced that you simply don't take
  the time.
- You may assume that having a good job should be
  reward enough.
- You may have a tendency to pay more attention to people
  with authority than to those who lack it.
- You may see praise and recognition as less important than
  your "real" leadership responsibilities.
- You may think that too much praise is coddling.
- You may think that people should naturally be motivated
  without a lot of external reinforcement.

Taking Action

Consider three ideas when it comes to letting people know that
you value them: engage, discover, and validate. First, take a lesson
from the Affirming leader and learn to **engage** people one-on-one
or in small group settings. Simply by taking the time to interact
with people, you show them that they matter to you. This can be
done organically or on some type of schedule—it just depends
on what's most comfortable for you. Next, **discover** why it is that
various people come to work each day. What are their personal
goals and dreams? What aspects of their work are most motivating
for them? Try to get a better sense of what makes people tick. We
think you'll find that most people like to talk about themselves!
Finally, take the time (and energy) to **validate** people for doing
good work. There are so many different ways to do this, but the
goal is pretty much the same: make them feel important and help
them to see that they're a key part of your team. If you can tell
them exactly *why* they're so valuable, that's even better. How do
you like to be recognized? That's a good starting point, but do
spend some time reflecting on the 8 Dimensions of Leadership
Model and thinking about the different types of recognition that
might work best for people with different styles.

Lesson Three: People Aren't Going to Act the Way You Think They Should

Affirming leaders don't assume that everyone does—or even should—see things their way. They have a genuine interest in understanding different perspectives and accommodating other people's ideas. Leaders who find the Affirming Dimension less natural often not only have high standards, but also have strong opinions about how things *should* be done. It may be very difficult for them to relate to other people's perspectives, and they may often feel they could do things more efficiently than most people. Less-than-Affirming leaders may be more concerned with either quality or speed, and it may be frustrating to watch people think just the opposite. Leaders whose styles fall on the western side of the model often build their opinions on how things should be done on their own biases toward logic, particularly *their* logic. Affirming leaders recognize that people don't always see things their way.

Big Suggestion Three: Accept Other People's Limitations

Affirming leaders accept other people's limitations and make them feel like valuable members of the group. There are many reasons why leaders who are less inclined toward the Affirming Dimension get caught up in how people "should" behave. If you struggle with this, what we're asking you to do is not going to be easy. We want you to accept that you may not have cornered the market on the only way to solve a problem. Creative solutions can come from anywhere and Affirming leaders understand that leading with the attitude that "all the good ideas come from me," or, "it's my way or the highway," have a chilling effect on creativity and innovation. People have their own opinions about methods or what constitutes a good job. Sometimes, their way may be as valid—or even more valid—than yours. Many times, not-so-Affirming leaders just aren't open to appreciating ideas that don't line up with what's in their own heads. Affirming leaders welcome other opinions and strive to facilitate dialogue around the differences.

Is It Worth It?

When you don't trust others to carry their load, you may waste a lot of energy worrying. When you can't see what people are doing, you may find it difficult to assume that they're doing things up to your standards. You may assume that they aren't doing it the way you would, and you know what? You may be right! It may be hard for you to watch others use methods that don't make sense to you, but you need to choose your battles. If the outcome is satisfactory—and it should be if you've made your expectations clear—giving people the autonomy to decide how to get there can be empowering for them.

If you try to control things too much, you allow people very little flexibility to work within their own strengths. Furthermore, when you stress out about how things are being done or mentally write people off as incompetent, people pick up on your disdain. As a result, they're likely to disengage. Most adults want some space to use their own skills and creativity to execute tasks. Sure, as a leader, it's your responsibility to help establish some basic processes and systems. But within those parameters, you need to give people the same freedom that you enjoy. Affirming leaders have a laid-back approach that gives people the benefit of the doubt. This empowers people to find their own path and to build their own problem-solving skills. Most importantly, it makes them feel competent.

Potential Obstacles to Accepting Other People's Limitations for Not-So-Affirming Leaders

- You may have a guarded posture toward life that makes it difficult to accept other people's apparent shortcomings.
- You may struggle to give up control over your tightly controlled worldview.

- You may honestly believe that there's no excuse for many "flaws" such as carelessness, procrastination, and lack of attention.
- You may hate to condone anything that seems to fall below your standards.
- You may have a clearly defined vision for how things should proceed.

Taking Action

Focus on three ideas when it comes to accepting other people's limitations: reflect, choose, and strive. First, **reflect** a bit on what you expect from other leaders. Most likely, you want direction and inspiration without micromanagement. Keep in mind that most people want to have some autonomy in their work. This helps them to feel important and needed. Keep this in the back of your mind as you work to be more appreciative of difference and less judgmental about people's methods. Next, **choose** your battles. Decide when you really need to step in. When you do have to correct something, practice a more tactful method of giving feedback, even if it feels contrived to you. When you have input to share with a colleague, challenge yourself to start and end with a positive comment. Finally, avoid being dismissive, and **strive** to understand the other person by asking questions until you understand exactly what's driving his or her opposition. If people give you input that you don't care for or understand, thank them for the suggestions and request that they send you an email with a few more details so you can process the idea. Be sure to follow up with them after you revisit your initial reactions and assumptions. When you find yourself becoming defensive about your ideas, take a step back. Use this as an opportunity to practice appreciating opposing viewpoints and taking them seriously.

Conclusion

Whatever your primary leadership dimension, it's valuable to adopt some of the Affirming leader's warm, inviting, and collaborative ways, even if ever so slightly. Specifically, to be more Affirming:

- Monitor your "default" expressions,
- Let people know that you value them, and
- Accept other people's limitations.

Case Study: Accept Other People's Limitations

We asked Wendy, a former leadership development executive at a Fortune 500 company, how she would coach her younger self to be a more effective leader. Earlier in her career, she worked in a healthcare setting where she struggled to lead a group of practitioners through a change. She wished she had done a few things differently. "First of all, asking questions, asking more questions to understand what was going on with people on my team and just really seeking to understand where they were in the change process and then helping them through that." She explained that as leader, it would have been helpful to know where everyone was on the change curve and to understand that everyone was probably in a different place. During this time of change, however, she hadn't had this insight. "Having conversations about that with them and trying to meet them where they were, as opposed to just ignor[ing] that and forg[ing] ahead. That would have made it hugely more successful from a personal point of view." Looking back, she now realizes the importance of accepting people's perceived limitations. Not everyone agreed with the changes that Wendy wanted to make and not everyone was comfortable doing things a new way. "I grew up in a very empirical PhD program," she joked, "and not everybody is an empiricist, you know. I mean it goes back to the same thing, I suppose, of really understanding the individual as an individual. And how can I meet them where they are? And together try to accomplish the mission, the goal."

Chapter 14

Lessons from Inclusive Leaders

What Can We Learn from Inclusive Leaders?

Whether you're highly Inclusive already or suspect that you may need to dial up this dimension, we'll give you a tour of this people-oriented approach. As we discussed in Chapter 2, the Inclusive approach is located in the southeastern area of the 8 Dimensions of Leadership Model, which means that Inclusive leaders tend to be cautious and reflective, as well as warm and accepting. In this chapter, we'll paint a picture of these leaders in action.

Inclusive leaders want to provide stability, to show concern for others, and more than anything, to maintain a harmonious environment. They tend to be soft-spoken, and they're more likely to lead by example than with force. In general, they do a lot more listening and thinking than speaking, and because they tend to be modest, they're careful not to impose on others. Inclusive leaders work carefully to make sure everything is done "just so," and they often shy away from radical changes and adventurous ideas. They're more concerned with being helpful and collaborative, and they're usually willing to go the extra mile for everyone.

There are many benefits to the Inclusive approach. These leaders care deeply about what other people think. They tend to be good listeners, and they're always open to other people's input. When people come to them with a problem or bad news, they handle the situation calmly and empathically, such that others see them as very approachable. Their down-to-earth style helps Inclusive leaders bring people together, and they're often quite good at drawing out people's opinions and helping a group reach consensus. Because they have lower ego needs, they're true team players who are more concerned with reaching goals collaboratively than with earning brownie points or getting ahead of the next person.

Strengths of Inclusive Leaders

- They tend to be very people-oriented.
- They're often able to create a warm, safe environment.
- They're able to overlook other people's flaws.
- They tend to deliver reliable results.
- They're often good listeners.
- They tend to be patient.
- They're willing to make compromises.
- They tend to show appreciation for others' contributions.

Inclusive leaders bring many gifts to their organizations. Through years of leader-watching and research, we've developed three essential lessons that Inclusive leaders have to offer. These three lessons are built around their tendency to seek harmony. If you're an Inclusive leader, these lessons should ring true to you. If you'd like to work on adding more of the Inclusive Dimension to your leadership practice, these three lessons and their complementary suggestions are a great place to start.

Three Essential Lessons from Inclusive Leaders

- There has never been a leader who succeeded without the support of others.
- Your words and emotions as a leader carry a lot of weight.
- Listening is easy to talk about but hard to do.

In this chapter, we'll explore these three lessons, point out some obstacles that not-so-Inclusive leaders might face, and offer suggestions for how to bring these lessons to life. Not all of the observations here will describe any one leader perfectly, but we think you'll gain some very useful insights into your fundamental assumptions and thought patterns around being Inclusive.

Lesson One: There Has Never Been a Leader Who Succeeded without the Support of Others

Inclusive leaders recognize that other people have great ideas, too. This one sounds pretty obvious, but there are many leaders out there who simply aren't very open to other people's ideas. This is particularly true of leaders who pride themselves on being able to pull themselves up by their bootstraps because they have a level of self-reliance that is sometimes not conducive to true collaboration. Not-so-Inclusive leaders have been known to act as though they could complete everyone's work, with better results, if only they had enough time. Leaders who are intensely competitive can often view themselves as a team of one, and on a subconscious level, they may feel driven to succeed entirely on their own as a matter of personal pride. With this mentality, it's easy to see how some leaders aren't open to—or interested in— other people's opinions.

Big Suggestion One: Show People That You're Open to Their Ideas

Inclusive leaders don't have high ego needs, so they don't care where the best ideas come from—they just want the group to come up with great ideas! People tend to feel comfortable bringing their ideas to Inclusive leaders, because even if the ideas don't get implemented, they'll be appreciated. Leaders who find the Inclusive Dimension less natural—often, but not always, those whose styles fall on the western side of the model—need to be more intentional about showing appreciation, because it simply doesn't feel as natural, or even necessary, to them. Their skepticism can shut people down, maybe even make people feel stupid for saying anything at all. Perhaps you feel that you *do* value people's input very much. Even if you do, they may not pick up on it because you simply don't make it clear.

Is It Worth It?

You may be wondering why you should bother putting more effort into this area. After all, you've gotten where you are today without giving this much thought. We'd like you to step back and consider, for a moment, your *own* needs. What can others do to acknowledge your ideas in a way that makes you feel good and inspires you to want to generate more? Looking back on your career—and your life in general—are there any patterns in the types of acknowledgement that tend to refuel you? In our experience, even people who are lower on the Inclusive Dimension want to have their ideas acknowledged. In fact, because they're often more ego-driven, they may have a high need in this area and enjoy being given credit for their big ideas in public.

One thing the 8 Dimensions of Leadership Model makes clear is that not all people have the same needs, but most people do want to be heard by their leaders. Some people have more to say than others, but they want their ideas to be acknowledged. If your goal as a leader is to help others be the best they can be— and hence, help create a better organization—this is essential. You need to get out of your own head and consider: What can I do to show others that I'm open to their ideas and that their contributions matter? The desire to be recognized is an innate human need—a need that you possess. It costs you nothing, and the ROI is substantial.

Potential Obstacles to Showing People That You're Open to
Their Ideas for Not-So-Inclusive Leaders

- You may get so caught up in your own vision that you can't
  see anything beyond it.
- You may be too busy talking to let people share their ideas.
- You may feel threatened or irritated by people who think
  they're better than you.
- You may have trouble taking people seriously if they're too
  enthusiastic.
- You may have little patience for people who seem hesitant
  to express their ideas
- You may not even realize that you aren't open to people's
  ideas.

Taking Action

If you remember anything about showing people that you're
open to their ideas, remember this: pause, acknowledge, and
attribute. First, **pause** momentarily to actually evaluate people's
ideas. Rejecting ideas outright without giving them consideration
shows a lack of respect. The pause can be ever so brief—just make
sure that you actually do *consider* the idea. Next, **acknowledge**
the idea, even if your initial reaction is that you can't stand it!
On our team, we make a point of using the "yes, and" method
wherein people build on each other's ideas rather than throwing
out the all-too-easy "yeah, but." It's easy to point out a million
reasons why someone's ideas won't work. Challenge yourself to
build on the ideas rather than simply dismissing them. At the
very least, acknowledge the person's effort. Finally, make a point
to **attribute** ideas and contributions to the appropriate sources.
If someone throws out an idea in a meeting that leads to a huge
improvement for the organization, let that person know that
you remember. Encourage people to keep up the good work, and
they're likely to contribute more good ideas down the road.

Lesson Two: Your Words and Emotions As a Leader Carry a Lot of Weight

Inclusive leaders choose their words carefully and err on the side of diplomacy. Once you're in any sort of position of power, people will pay more attention to not only your words, but your body language as well. Many intense leaders—typically those whose styles fall on the western and northern sides of the model—often recognize that they have a certain edge, but they may vastly underestimate the impact that their intensity has on other people. For instance, your words and actions may seem fairly harmless in your own mind, but to others, they can come across as combative or demoralizing. When people perceive that you are indifferent or even hostile toward them, it can erode loyalty to both you as a leader and the organization.

Big Suggestion Two: Monitor Your Emotional Output Carefully

As a leader, you're in a powerful position, and people pick up on your moods more than you may realize. A slight roll of your eyes or an exaggerated sigh may get replayed over and over again in the mind of someone who seeks to please you. Expressions of anger or irritation (e.g., a raised voice, a blunt response), can have an even more devastating impact. Generally speaking, when a leader gives off a lot of negative emotions, it creates a stressful environment where people constantly question their standing. People whose styles fall on the southern side of the model may really struggle in this type of environment, as they have a higher need for stability. Sure, many people need to feel a little pressure to perform at their best, but there's a big difference between a culture of urgency and a culture of fear.

Is It Worth It?

Many not-so-Inclusive leaders may think people shouldn't take things so personally. Maybe you agree—they need to toughen up. This is a case where it may be helpful to refer back to the 8 Dimensions of Leadership Model. People whose styles fall on the eastern side of the model tend to be accepting and warm, and they often feel extremely uncomfortable with negative emotions. If you're a leader who is generally comfortable with conflict, this may be difficult for you to grasp. For people who see the world through a more optimistic, accepting lens, negative emotions can actually pose quite a threat. In fact, your negativity can even derail their productivity. However, showing diplomacy takes thoughtfulness, and this requires more time and energy. It involves putting yourself in the other person's shoes and imagining their reaction. Then it involves choosing the words that convey your meaning without ticking people off. All this takes effort, and it's no wonder that some people think, "To hell with it—I'm just going to blurt it out."

As a leader, one of your jobs is to create an environment that enables people to do their best work. Now, as we've discussed, people have a wide variety of needs and preferences when it comes to what motivates them. Guess what? *Nobody* will be in a position to do their best work if you can't monitor and control your negative emotions. You may think it's their problem if they "can't take it," but in reality, it's your problem, too. Callousness has the power to erode trust, loyalty, motivation, and engagement. To be a great leader, you not only have to *show* concern for the people you lead, but you also must *have* genuine concern for them.

Potential Obstacles to Monitoring Your Emotional Output for Not-So-Inclusive Leaders

- You may think it takes a lot less energy to simply say what's on your mind.
- You may resent the idea that people expect diplomacy.
- You may get caught up in how things should go and respond very poorly when they don't.

- You may not be a particularly patient person.
- You may have trouble filtering your words.
- You may be in such a hurry that you don't have time for diplomacy.

Taking Action

To monitor your emotional output more carefully, do the following: connect, relate, and channel. If you're highly driven, you may often breeze past people without really acknowledging their presence, especially when you're upset. Make a conscientious effort to **connect** with people personally, even if it's just making eye contact and nodding. By acknowledging them as human beings, it will be a lot easier to communicate. Secondly, **relate** to the other person's perspective. Hear your words from their perspective. Anticipate how they'll interpret what's coming out of your mouth. Be forewarned, however, that this takes a lot more time, energy, and practice than it might seem. Finally, work to **channel** any irritation you may feel toward others into constructive criticism rather than speaking too bluntly and saying something you might regret. If you have high standards—and many leaders do—you *will* get irritated, but you *can* choose to use that energy in a more productive way. Remember, your words and emotions as a leader carry a lot of weight.

Lesson Three: Listening is Easy to Talk about but Hard to Do

Many people think they're great listeners, but listening really is easier said than done. Inclusive leaders have a patient, supportive style that makes them well suited to *actually* listen. They *actually* want to hear what the other person is saying. They're not pretending. As a culture, we often put an emphasis on the great speaker—the larger-than-life person who can captivate an audience and gain people's buy-in. It's true that charisma can go a long way toward leadership success. However, the great listener should also be revered. Leaders who truly listen gain important information from the people who sometimes know more—or at least know different pieces of information—about the organization than the leaders themselves. Not only does listening help leaders gather good information, but it goes a long way toward building trust and respect.

Big Suggestion Three: Work to Facilitate Two-Way Discussion on Important Issues

Inclusive leaders aren't the most forceful people in the world, so when big issues come up, they may not pull people together with urgency or an inspirational speech, but they are great at inviting people to be involved in the conversation. When decisions need to be made, they actually want people's input, and they make an effort to seek it out. They aren't threatened by other people's contributions, and they see real value in gaining multiple perspectives. Because they aren't likely to get caught up in the emotions of the issue, they can facilitate a fair, calm discussion. These highly collaborative leaders like to make decisions as a group when possible, and this may be counterintuitive to some leaders who are more autonomous.

Is It Worth It?

One Pioneering leader told us, "As I've matured, I've grown more tolerant, more accepting, and less critical. I've learned to listen more and facilitate better. My advice would be to acquire these characteristics earlier." What are the benefits of being able to facilitate two-way discussion on important issues? First and foremost, it makes people feel like they're part of the team—and they are, right? It's true that you won't always want to involve everyone in every decision you make, but there are plenty of times when facilitating some dialogue around an issue would be not only appropriate, but quite helpful.

As we've discussed, one of the main reasons to seek out the involvement of others is that they may actually know some things that you don't know! A novel concept, right? They experience your organization and your group differently than you do, and their perspectives could tip you off to something you hadn't considered before. So we're telling you that you don't have to have all of the answers, and that by reaching out to other people, you'll gain insights and make people feel important. Most fundamentally, you actually have to learn how to *value* the ideas of other people. Listening will never evolve beyond a painful chore to you unless you actually value what you're hearing.

Potential Obstacles to Facilitating Two-Way Discussion on Important Issues for Not-So-Inclusive Leaders

- You may not want to take the time to involve others.
- You may not realize that others would even want to be part of the discussion.
- You may feel like it would be a hassle to get people up to speed.
- You may think it would be better to just let people know once decisions have been made.
- You may prefer to divide and conquer rather than tying up everyone's time in a lot of meetings.
- You may not think that people would have anything all that valuable to offer.

Taking Action

To facilitate two-way discussion on important issues, we encourage you to do the following: invite, relax, and wait. First, **invite** diverse groups of people to the table. Mix things up a bit from time to time. For example, there may be initiatives where cross-departmental discussion could generate some great ideas. People are generally interested in sharing their viewpoints, so as long as you aren't calling meetings for the sake of having meetings, most will want to be involved. Next, **relax** your presence in the discussion. There's a real difference between leading a discussion and facilitating one. As a facilitator, your job is to encourage members of the group to share—not to do most of the sharing or to guide the discussion on a rigid path. Try to maintain a little distance from the discussion. Be an observer more than a participant. Those whose styles fall on the northern side of the model may struggle with this. Finally, **wait** longer than you think necessary before speaking. When there's a lull in conversation, let it ride for a few moments. Some of the more reserved members of your group may never speak if you're always jumping in with the next question. Give people the time and space they need to contribute.

Conclusion

Regardless of your primary leadership dimension, it's valuable to adopt some of the Inclusive leader's patient, accommodating, and even-tempered ways, even if ever so slightly. Specifically, to be more Inclusive:

- Show people that you're open to their ideas,
- Monitor your emotional output carefully, and
- Work to facilitate two-way discussion on important issues.

Case Study: Show People That You're Open to Their Ideas

Bettina, a Resolute leader and higher education administrator, learned that she needed to take more time to listen. Early on in her career, she got caught up in her own voice so much that she really wasn't hearing what others said. Like many leaders, she still struggles with this at times. "When I'm in a meeting," she explained, "I have to stop the voice inside my head—I literally have to stop it—from planning what I think should be said next and force myself to listen to the conversation." We asked her what benefits she sees when she does make the effort to listen. "[I'm] actually hearing what other people say and learning. You know, the wisdom of the crowd is amazing," she said. Bettina has been able to grow in this area, but it hasn't always been easy. "I have to stop. It's almost a mantra— to stop, breathe, and say to myself, 'Listen. Really, you'll enjoy it. You'll *learn* something,'" she laughed. "You know, and then I do. And, then I'm engaged and it's really a treat, like having dessert. It's fun." For Bettina, learning to be more collaborative has revealed a new reality in which people actually do better work together. Like many leaders, Bettina often has a strong vision for how things should go, and doing things collaboratively doesn't always mean getting to the exact same place she initially imagined. "But [working collaboratively] gets [the group] to the place that we all want to go," she said. "It's curious because I find that the crowd ends up molding— modeling maybe—a different endpoint, but it's an endpoint that I'm pretty darn comfortable with almost all the time." As a leader who values personal competence, she didn't realize how much her tendency to want to control the conversation was actually a burden. By learning to engage others in dialogue and do things more collaboratively, she actually reduced her load. "It's letting go of this burden that you've been carrying on your shoulders, thinking that you have to do it all by yourself your whole life," she explained.

Chapter 15

Lessons from Humble Leaders

What Can We Learn from Humble Leaders?

Whether you've determined that you're a Humble leader or you feel that you need to become a more Humble leader, we'll help you explore this important dimension of leadership in more detail. As we discussed in Chapter 2, the Humble Dimension is located on the southern side of the 8 Dimensions of Leadership Model, which means that Humble leaders tend to be cautious and reflective. Their modest, internal nature belies a number of very powerful leadership skills. And although individual Humble leaders have many unique traits that set them apart, we've found predictable patterns—we know what makes these leaders tick.

Humble leaders want to support the people around them, to ensure accurate results, and more than anything, to provide reliable leadership. Harmony is important to them, both in terms of tasks and relationships. They tend to be diplomatic, soft-spoken leaders, and they don't often wear their emotions on their sleeves. They're conscientious about getting things right and are willing to take the extra time to nail down the details. In fact, they can be quite perfectionistic at times. At their core, Humble leaders want to be seen as reliable. They have a penchant for routine and consistency, and they maximize predictability by relying heavily on their past experiences.

There are many benefits to this Humble Dimension. Humble leaders have a steady, consistent way of creating a culture where quality is expected. They also strive to create a stable environment where people know what to expect on a day-to-day basis, and they tend to be good at maintaining their composure, even under stress. Our research suggests that providing a sense of stability is, in fact, the behavior most highly correlated with being respected as a good leader in the organization. Because of these traits, Humble leaders often have long tenures at organizations. Therefore, they're often seen as dependable, go-to leaders. And, because they aren't caught up in their own ego needs, they tend to be fair-minded leaders who try to make careful decisions that will benefit everyone.

Strengths of Humble Leaders

- They're often able to head off potential problems with careful planning.
- They provide others with the tools necessary to do their work.
- They're able to create a stable environment.
- They maintain their composure, even under stress.
- They're conscientious about reaching closure on projects and initiatives.
- They model a steady work ethic.
- They expect themselves and others to deliver accurate outcomes.

Humble leaders have many admirable leadership qualities to offer to their organizations and to the world. Through years of leader-watching and research, we've developed three essential lessons that Humble leaders have to offer. These three lessons highlight Humble leaders' core desires for security, peacefulness, and fairness. If you consider yourself a Humble leader, we think these lessons will validate the way you currently carry yourself as a leader. If, on the other hand, you need to dial up the Humble Dimension, these three lessons and their complementary suggestions will help you grow as a leader.

Three Essential Lessons from Humble Leaders

- People need leaders to stay calm under fire.
- You need other people more than you think.
- Other people have needs that differ from your own.

In this chapter, we'll explore these three lessons, dig into the obstacles that not-so-Humble leaders might face, and offer suggestions for how to bring these lessons to life. Not all of the observations here will describe any one leader perfectly, but we think you'll gain some very useful insights into your fundamental assumptions and thought patterns around being Humble.

Lesson One: People Need Leaders to Stay Calm under Fire

Humble leaders are self-controlled people who are good at staying calm and keeping an even keel, even when things get difficult. Many leaders struggle to maintain their composure when things don't go according to plan, when people drop the ball, or when bad news is delivered. For leaders, things can seem quite serious in the moment, and it's easy to let emotions boil over, sometimes over relatively inconsequential problems. Leaders who have a tendency to lose their cool can learn a thing or two from Humble leaders about keeping things in perspective.

Big Suggestion One: Maintain Your Composure by Keeping Things in Perspective

In our research, one Commanding leader told us that she wished she'd known sooner to just take a deep breath and calm down when things get rocky. As she put it, "In retrospect, things are not as serious as they seem in the moment." This is easier said than done, particularly for the fast-paced leaders who tend to react to situations quickly. Humble leaders aren't in a hurry to make decisions. They want to ensure that their choices will have the desired effect *right now*, but also down the road. Because they tend to be more methodical about problem-solving, they don't pressure themselves to make immediate decisions. They also tend to be fair-minded and modest, so they have an easier time taking their ego out of the equation. They simply work as efficiently as they can to resolve the issues in the best interest of everyone involved.

Is It Worth It?

Most of us lose our tempers from time to time, but what happens when this becomes a regular occurrence? Frankly, people find it unnerving to see leaders in panic mode. People look to leaders for strength and guidance, and if the leader seems out of control, the panic can be contagious. In addition, when a leader takes setbacks or bad news personally, people may put off sharing things with the leader for fear of their reaction. When not-so-Humble leaders consistently fly off the handle or become moody, they may be the last ones to know about problems in the group, and this can be costly. In an ideal world, mistakes are opportunities to learn and grow, but this isn't the case if people face threatening consequences such as intense emotional backlash.

What are the benefits of maintaining perspective—and your composure—when under fire? There are two that stand out: You're better able to make sound, well-thought-out decisions, and you're less likely to alienate other people. Both are extremely important. By keeping things in perspective, you allow yourself to think beyond the here-and-now and consider what you know from past experience, what might happen tomorrow, and where you want to guide the group down the road. You can step back to look at the big picture, to see things from other people's perspectives, and to play the devil's advocate. Essentially, you give yourself the space to make better decisions. By maintaining your composure, you not only avoid frightening people, but you model self-control and respect.

Potential Obstacles to Maintaining Your Composure by Keeping Things in Perspective for Not-So-Humble Leaders

- You may be an impatient person.
- You may be extremely emotionally invested in what you do.
- You may be so competitive that you can't stand the thought of losing.
- You may have exceedingly high standards for yourself and others.
- You may be uncomfortable with chaos.
- You may not really care who's in your way when you're trying to resolve problems.
- You may be inclined to see criticism or disagreement as an attack.

Taking Action

We'd like you to consider three ideas when it comes to maintaining your composure by keeping things in perspective: find, test, and recruit. First, **find** another outlet for your fear and anger. Do not give yourself the luxury of unleashing your unfiltered emotion on bystanders just because you can. We're not saying that you shouldn't hold people accountable or share your frustration about disappointments. We're suggesting that if you have a tendency to lose your composure in a less-than-constructive way, it may help to filter those feelings through another outlet first. Your outlet can be unique to you—explore different methods such as talking things out with a trusted colleague, getting some fresh air, meditating, or even doing something more physical like getting in a quick workout or yoga practice. Next, **test** your assumptions about the crisis in the grand scheme of things. What aspects of the situation can you control? What aspects are outside of your control entirely? How can you break down the problem into manageable pieces? What should be done first? What's really going to matter next week? Next year? Once you've removed some of the emotional intensity, it should be a lot easier to take stock of the real issues. Finally, **recruit** any help you need to get back on track. Don't be a martyr or try to save the day. It's not about blame or credit—it's about doing right by the organization. Use your leadership skills to tackle the problem as a team.

Lesson Two: You Need Other People More Than You Think

Part of a leader's job is to empower people—all people—and Humble leaders are great at showing modesty and making people count. Leaders who are low on the Humble Dimension may pour too much of their empowerment energy into giving inspirational speeches and promoting their own vision. Their communication is often a one-way street, and after they've delivered their message, they're not always there to offer support to people. Eventually, people start to feel that the not-so-Humble leaders they work with aren't really interested in listening to them. If leaders don't show a certain degree of modesty, they can lose followers along the way. And not only do leaders need their followers to help execute their visions, but the followers often have valuable opinions to share. Humble leaders are good at taking the time to listen to the people around them—even those in lower-level positions.

Big Suggestion Two: Take the Time to Listen to the Less Powerful People around You

Leaders who are low on the Humble Dimension often don't take the time to hear what's being said at all levels of the organization. This may be true for a variety of reasons—lack of interest, egotism, lack of time, or a tendency to be private or detached.

Whatever the reason, not taking the time to listen sends the same basic message: a lack of respect or consideration for the very people who are needed to carry out the vision. If you're a little lower than you'd like to be on the Humble Dimension, we encourage you to dig deep and reflect on this recommendation to be more attentive to those who are less powerful in your organization.

Is It Worth It?

Let's explore the benefits of taking the time to listen more often. This simple action does many things to improve your leadership effectiveness. First and foremost, it empowers people. This helps you build alignment, creates a greater sense of autonomy for others, and shows your more vulnerable side. People will almost always be grateful that you spent time listening to them, and it's a simple way to make them feel important. If you're low on the Humble Dimension, chances are good that you can relate to wanting to feel important. So think about the benefits you could provide to others by making *them* feel like a vital part of the organization. While it may seem contradictory, building up other people can actually increase your own personal power.

Not only does taking the time to listen make people feel good, but it keeps you in touch with the inner workings of your organization. You can pick up crucial information that you're simply going to miss if you spend all of your time managing up, crunching numbers, or working with external clients. When you show others that you value their opinions and experiences, they feel more comfortable coming to you with problems and suggestions. As a leader, you don't want to be in a position where you're the last to hear that trouble is brewing. Humble leaders tend to be self-controlled and steady, and people at all levels of the organization often feel that they're fair-minded when it comes to listening to people's concerns.

Potential Obstacles to Listening to Less Powerful People for Not-So-Humble Leaders

- You may be outgoing and have a tendency to want to speak rather than listen.
- You may question the competency of people who aren't assertive with their opinions.
- You may have trouble letting go of your own vision to see value in other people's ideas.
- Your radar may be more attuned to the "important" people around you.
- It may be difficult for you to see beyond someone's lack of personal power to recognize their good ideas.
- It may be taxing for you to spend the time and emotional energy needed to listen to and empathize with people.

Taking Action

Focus on three ideas when it comes to taking the time to listen to the less powerful people around you: reflect, create, and listen. First, **reflect** on what you have to gain by truly listening to people at all levels of your organization. Sure, we've listed some benefits here, but what about for you personally? What might you learn? How might listening help you reach your goals? Next, **create** the time and space that you'll need to give this the attention it deserves. Maybe you can fit it in here and there, in casual bits and pieces. Or, maybe you'll need to create more structure for yourself to ensure that you do this. For example, you could schedule monthly, quarterly, or yearly meetings, or even meals, with certain groups of people. Do whatever it takes to create a plan that will help you hold yourself accountable. Finally, **listen!** That's right—spend a lot more time listening than talking. Sure, it can be helpful to ask specific questions, but make sure to give people the time to respond before jumping in to help them along. If you make a concerted effort to talk less, you may just realize how much you've been monopolizing conversations.

Show people that you appreciate their perspectives. It will go a long way toward making them feel empowered.

Lesson Three: Other People Have Needs That Differ from Your Own

Humble leaders recognize that other people have needs that differ from their own, and the rest of us can learn something from these fair-minded leaders. Many leaders are great at showing passion and exploring new territory but fail to address the internal needs of the group. They spend a lot of energy convincing others to get on board with their visions, but they may not take the time to understand the needs of their people. When leaders who are low on the Humble Dimension are busy pursuing their own goals, other people may feel like they're simply being dragged along for the ride. The danger of this egocentric point of view is that by expecting people to adapt to your vision, you may lose touch with the evolving needs of the group.

Big Suggestion Three: Make the Needs of Your Group a Priority

Sure, leaders can often get by with the luxury of having people cater to *their* needs. But in the long run, gaining alignment and getting the best from people requires you to pay attention to everyone's needs—especially those of the people below you. In some ways, this may feel like a burden, and it might be a relief to drop this responsibility and simply focus on your own needs and goals. Isn't that one of the perks of being on top? Perhaps, but that's not leadership. Not everyone shares your worldview, and to create a culture that works for everyone, you'll need to pay more attention to other people's needs.

Is It Worth It?

When you operate as an individual—if that's ever entirely possible—you can explore the world unencumbered. As a leader, you can't do this. You have to bring other people along on your journey. In fact, it's no longer "your" journey, and in some respects, this will slow you down. You can choose to look at this as baggage, or you can see this as an opportunity to take on a whole new role. The transition from individual contributor to leader is a little bit like becoming a parent. You give up some of your freedom as you gain responsibility. The same is true of leadership, and followers have many needs, many of which may seem a little foreign to you.

For example, many of your followers may have a high need for security, and this means that rapid change will be difficult—if not downright disconcerting—for them. Depending on your leadership style, this may be a little tough for you to understand. Many leaders enjoy the variety that change provides, particularly those leaders whose styles fall on the northern side of the model. However, many good, valuable people care more about security than adventure. Likewise, many people have different information needs than you do. Many leaders who focus less on the Humble Dimension fail to provide a comprehensive picture of the state of affairs. Rather, news tends to trickle down to people slowly, and this can leave people feeling in the dark and insecure. Another example is that some people have different quality standards than you. Perhaps you take a fast-paced approach that doesn't always allow more conscientious people the time to achieve the quality results they need to feel good about their work and themselves. These are just a few examples of the kinds of needs that people on your team may have, and it's absolutely worth your time to make these needs a priority.

Potential Obstacles to Making the Needs of Your Group a Priority for Not-So-Humble Leaders

- You may assume that what's good for you must be good for other people.
- You may assume that when other people nod their heads, they must be entirely on board.
- You may naturally focus on convincing others to see your point of view.

- You may not see the value in seeking input from people who don't have as much power as you.
- You may not feel like you have the time to focus on meeting people's needs.
- You may be more autonomous than collaborative.

Taking Action

We'd like you to consider three ideas when it comes to making the needs of your group a priority: appreciate, balance, and check. First, learn to **appreciate** the styles that differ from your own, then try to anticipate the needs and limitations that might come with them. Use the 8 Dimensions of Leadership Model as a starting point. For example, consider the needs of people whose approaches sit opposite yours on the model. People may require more or less structure than you do. Next, **balance** the needs of your group or organization. Be fair-minded about how you prepare people for upcoming changes. When planning your communication, design it to meet the needs of everyone in the group, keeping in mind that some are often more informed than others. What information might people be missing? How do your plans tie into the big picture? What obstacles might people face? Finally, **check** the emotional pulse of the people you lead on a regular basis. Are they anxious, exhausted, confused, or checked out? Don't assume that people will bring problems to you. From time to time, directly ask people what they need to be more effective in their roles. Taking the time to do this may be difficult, but your group is likely to be more engaged and productive if they see you as a fair, considerate leader.

Conclusion

Whatever your primary leadership dimension, we think it's valuable to adopt some of the Humble leader's modest, careful, self-controlled, and soft-spoken ways, even if ever so slightly. Specifically, to be more Humble:

- Maintain your composure by keeping things in perspective,

- Take the time to listen to the less powerful people around you, and
- Make the needs of your group a priority.

Case Study: Maintain Your Composure by Keeping Things in Perspective and Take the Time to Listen to the Less Powerful People Around You

We talked to Steve, a marketing consultant and former VP at several consumer goods companies, about the most valuable leadership lessons he has learned. "Really be conscious that the minute you feel stressed, your worst attributes will show," he said. "Hey, you know it's going to happen, and that's when I've found that I'm least able to control my natural impulses, is when I'm under stress." When situations became stressful, Steve often overlooked the ideas and needs of others and just did whatever it took to get results. Today, he has more perspective on the importance of humility—especially when under pressure. When he worked for a large resort company early in his career, he had a great mentor who embodied the Humble Dimension. "I had a boss that really got it," he said. "It was interesting because in many ways, he was probably wired like me." Steve is a Pioneering leader, and he thought his boss was extremely sharp. "His favorite thing to do was to get up at five in the morning and go into the break room with the maids and the janitors at the resort," he said. "He would sit and have coffee and donuts with them and just talk about their family and their life. He loved it. He didn't do it because he was going through the motions." While Steve's boss really enjoyed this social time with his workers, he was also able to hear exactly what was and wasn't working at the resort, and this information helped him to do his job better. By valuing his workers as people, he not only made them feel good, but he was able to make better decisions. Steve's boss encouraged him to do the same with the people he managed. Steve found that it was sometimes difficult, but he definitely saw the value in taking the time to listen to the less powerful around him.

Chapter 16

Lessons from Deliberate Leaders

What Can We Learn from Deliberate Leaders?

Deliberate leaders take a measured approach to their work. They're not about the immediate payoff and making a big spectacle of themselves. Using logic and carefully designed systems, they take the time necessary to get things right. Whether you think of yourself as a Deliberate leader or quite the opposite, we'll give you a good sense of this analytical approach. As we discussed in Chapter 2, the Deliberate Dimension is located in the southwestern area of the 8 Dimensions of Leadership Model, which means that these leaders tend to be cautious and reflective, as well as questioning and skeptical. We'll explore some key qualities that Deliberate leaders have to offer.

Deliberate leaders want to create a sense of stability, to solve problems, and more than anything, to ensure accurate outcomes. They like to have a plan, and they'd much rather over-prepare than risk failure. Personal competency matters to them, and they want to be seen as having expertise in their field. Because they're analytical leaders who communicate in a straightforward manner, they may have little patience for people who seem illogical or more interested in schmoozing than getting work done. They tend to be reserved, and when interacting with people socially, they often prefer intimate groups to large parties or professional networking opportunities.

Organizations rely on Deliberate leaders to deliver a well-crafted product—whether that product is an actual object, intellectual property, or a service. The little things matter to Deliberate leaders, and colleagues rely on them to create an environment where people know what to expect. Deliberate leaders possess an even temper, and they enjoy helping people with problems related to processes and systems. Deliberate leaders aren't afraid of the ambiguity involved in solving a complex problem—in fact, they welcome the opportunity to make sense of it. Here are just a few of the Deliberate leader's strengths.

Strengths of Deliberate Leaders

- They're determined to get things done right.
- They're often able to separate emotions from facts.
- They take the time to create systems and structures.
- They're not afraid to question ideas that seem illogical.
- They're comfortable working autonomously.
- They're able to work tirelessly to solve problems.
- They usually provide solid evidence for their arguments.

To the degree that organizations suffer from a lack of ability to execute on great ideas, Deliberate leaders may save the day. We've developed three essential lessons that Deliberate leaders have to offer. These three lessons are built around their tendencies to focus on specifics and clear communication. If you see yourself as a Deliberate leader, these lessons should affirm much of what you already do. Or, if you feel that more deliberateness could enhance your leadership practice, use these three lessons and their complementary suggestions as a starting point.

Three Essential Lessons from Deliberate Leaders

- People can't read your mind.
- The dots won't magically connect themselves.
- Leaders are responsible for ensuring that processes run smoothly.

In this chapter, we'll explore these three lessons, dig into the obstacles that not-so-Deliberate leaders might face, and offer suggestions for how to bring these lessons to life. Not all of the observations here will describe any one leader perfectly, but we think you'll gain some very useful insights into your fundamental assumptions and thought patterns around being Deliberate.

Lesson One: People Can't Read Your Mind

Deliberate leaders are often associated with language that is very precise, overly detailed, and somewhat formal or stilted. They speak with measured precision and choose words carefully. And while that form of communication may not inspire us to charge up a hill at the risk of great personal sacrifice, we always know where Deliberate leaders stand on an issue and the logic that informs their positions.

Many leaders who find the Deliberate Dimension less natural think of themselves as good communicators, simply because they are often social. And in many ways, they are good at communicating. They are open to other people, mingle easily, and tend to get lost in conversations. However, these leaders have some tendencies that make truly clear communication less likely. In general, they assume that people are more similar to them than they actually are. As a result, they often imagine a false sense of consensus. That is, they think people are on board, when in reality, they aren't. Their information may feel scattered, with updates relayed in a piecemeal fashion, and people may not grasp what their actual plan is.

Big Suggestion One: Be Deliberate in Your Communication

Deliberate leaders have something to teach us about forming and delivering a clear message. Their messages have structure that people can hold onto. This type of communication takes work (It's called deliberate for a reason!). Now, don't get us wrong—in many ways, all leaders are very skilled at connecting with people. But we're not talking about connecting; we're talking about forming and delivering a clear message.

Is It Worth It?

Sure, there's a time and a place for low-key, fun communication. We get that. But there are many times when a leader needs to create alignment by sending one clear, easily understood message. This helps people to feel that they're all headed in the same direction. People whose approaches fall on the southern side of the model often require a sense of stability, and by giving them more specific information, you can help them feel comfortable with upcoming changes.

Many times, leaders get so caught up in an exciting new direction that they forget to tell others that they've changed course. Intellectually, you certainly realize that people can't read your mind, but you may forget at times, and this can be frustrating for people, especially if you're a leader who tends to change directions frequently. Chances are good that you make a point to keep yourself "in the loop" as much as possible, and you need to make a point to bring others up to speed as well. It simply may not occur to you to slow down and reach out to others with the appropriate information. When leaders who are lower on the Deliberate Dimension do this on a regular basis, people may see them as reckless or unreliable.

Potential Obstacles to Communicating Deliberately for
Not-So-Deliberate Leaders

- You may have a tendency to juggle many different projects and ideas in your mind at once.

- You may simply not be very communicative.

- You may get so excited about ideas that you tend to focus on the big picture and don't provide enough detail.

- You may be quite talkative and use a stream-of-consciousness communication style.

- You may be so wrapped up in moving forward that you forget that your decisions impact others.

- You may not have a clear vision of where you're headed.

Taking Action

Consider three ideas when it comes to being more deliberate in your communication: empathize, establish, and pace. First, **empathize** with others who may require more clarity. When in doubt, assume that others need a little bit of background information before diving into your latest plan. When communicating a change, consider which aspects of the situation could cause fear and anxiety, and be sure to address these issues. Next, be sure to **establish** a main point and refer back to it regularly. Particularly when speaking to a large group, it's important to make your points systematically. It may feel a little elementary, especially if you're comfortable speaking, but spending a little more time laying out your points will go a long way toward promoting clarity and comprehension. Finally, **pace** yourself to balance action with communication. If you tend to move at a particularly fast pace, you may need to slow down to bring others along for the ride. If people feel like they're being left behind, it can be frustrating. When you're particularly excited about a new idea, make sure that you aren't getting too far ahead of others.

Lesson Two: The "Dots" Won't Magically Connect Themselves

Deliberate leaders cause their organizations to do the hard work of analysis. They demand preparation and require themselves and others to do their "homework" rather than relying on gut impressions. They don't just assume or hope that things will naturally work themselves out—they *make sure* that things are going to work out. Deliberate leaders promote disciplined analysis in their organizations, and this leadership behavior is requested frequently by many people who work for Energizing, Pioneering, and Commanding leaders. These fast-paced leaders are often so eager to move forward that the analysis sometimes falls by the wayside.

Big Suggestion Two: Show That You've Done Your Homework (and Really Do It)

Deliberate leaders demonstrate that in order to become more effective in advancing organizational initiatives, you need to show that you've done your homework. Maybe you're already doing it—or maybe you're not—but one thing is clear: you need to *show* others that you've done it. People want to see that your ideas can be substantiated. Sure, many people initially respond to high energy, but they may begin to grow suspicious if your ideas seem to be all talk. Not only is showing that you've done your analysis a matter of building your credibility, but it's a matter of making good decisions.

Is It Worth It?

Sure, passion can take you far as a leader, but if your results are less than optimal due to poor planning, you'll never gain credibility. You may be quite comfortable making changes on the fly—especially if your style falls on the northern end of the model—but this may feel very inefficient to others, causing them to wonder, "Why didn't we do it the right way from the start?" When leaders show that they've done their homework before charging ahead, people have more confidence in their ideas, and they can feel good about how their time is being spent. Nobody wants to waste their time following through on an ill-conceived plan.

By showing that you've done the research or analysis, others can see that your decisions aren't just made on a whim. They're able to trust that there is substance behind your decisions, and this makes you seem more competent as a leader. If you instinctively use a lot of enthusiasm to sell your ideas, keep in mind that to reach people whose styles fall on the western end of the model, you'll need to back up your optimism with some hard facts. By doing your homework before presenting your ideas, you can earn the trust of people who tend to be more analytical.

Potential Obstacles to Showing That You've Done Your Homework for Not-So-Deliberate Leaders

- You may have a tendency to focus on the big picture.
- You may speak impulsively and share your ideas before they're well formed.
- Your attention may often be pulled in multiple directions.
- You may enjoy starting new things a lot more than following through with the details.
- You may simply dislike drudging through deep analysis.
- You may be naturally inclined to sell ideas with enthusiasm rather than data.

Taking Action

Focus on three ideas when it comes to showing that you've done your homework: focus, gather, and explain. First, slow down and **focus** your energy on one important idea at a time. Sure, you can let the ideas fly as you're coming up with them, but consider being more selective about what ideas you actually present to others. When you've identified an idea that seems viable, do whatever it takes to **gather** information that will help you sell it to others. You can reach out to others for help, but make sure that you can show on paper how and why your plans will work. Play the devil's advocate with your information and make sure that it will stand up to lots of scrutiny. Most importantly, if you notice a pattern of evidence that suggests some weakness in your idea, go back to the drawing board. Once you've got an idea that's backed with solid support, **explain** it to others with more specificity than seems necessary. If you have a tendency to focus on the big picture, you'll need to be intentional about reiterating your main points and showing clearly that you've done your due diligence.

Lesson Three: Leaders Are Responsible for Ensuring That Processes Run Smoothly

One of a leader's responsibilities is to ensure that management issues are addressed. These can often be delegated, but there are many process-related areas in which leaders need to get their hands dirty. Leaders who are low on the Deliberate Dimension often have some tendencies that cause them to overlook these responsibilities, and even when they are aware of them, they may seem very unpleasant. In particular, leaders whose styles fall on the northern side of the model are often so interested in pushing forward that they allow the inner workings of the organization to get a little rusty. Because they have such a strong bias toward action, they don't always spend a lot of time observing, listening, and asking questions, and, when they get attached to an idea, they often find it difficult to process information that contradicts their train of thought.

Big Suggestion Three: Pay Attention to Process Management Tools and Methods

If you're a not-so-Deliberate leader, too much structure may seem stifling to you, and you may hate the idea of creating any unnecessary red tape. If this is the case, we're not suggesting that you give up your more flexible ways entirely—especially if you're a pioneer at heart! However, as a leader, you are responsible for creating an environment or a culture—a space in which other people can be successful in helping you work toward a shared vision. To create an effective space in which to do this, some structure is required, and sometimes more than you're naturally inclined to provide.

Is It Worth It?

Let's explore the benefits of paying attention to process management tools and methods. Daily maintenance of processes and systems is vital for creating a sense of stability for the people in your organization. If your eye is always on the horizon, waiting for the next exciting opportunity, it's difficult to make daily maintenance a priority. Addressing inefficiencies certainly isn't sexy, and it may not seem to promise much in the way of major gains. On the contrary, it often requires messy analytical work that, even if successful, will only get you where you think you *should* have been in the first place. There is nothing exciting about this, so it's easy to let inefficiencies slide when good enough will do. Much of the time, leaders who struggle in this area overlook less than ideal methods in the mentality of the 80/20 rule.

Sure, the 80/20 rule is absolutely called for at times. It helps you prioritize what needs to happen now, make timely decisions, and avoid getting caught up in overanalysis. However, if used too often at the expense of managing processes and methods, it can take a toll on more than just productivity. People begin to burn out when they see that a high percentage of their time is wasted. When an organization doesn't feel stable or "tight," it can have a negative impact on morale. This is especially true for those people who care a great deal about quality, and they may stop taking as much pride in their work. If you struggle with processes, your main goal may be something more like moving ahead at lightning speed, but many people find different types of satisfaction in their work—not only in achieving quality results, but also in knowing exactly what they're supposed to be doing and why.

Potential Obstacles to Paying Attention to Process Management Tools and Processes for Not-So-Deliberate Leaders

- You may be more interested in playing the role of doer (or idea-generator) than learner.
- You may be uncomfortable with the pain of working through the really entrenched problems.
- You may find it challenging to slow down and really understand logistics.
- You may think it's more interesting to operate in the world of possibilities than in reality.
- You may have a tendency to grow restless.
- You may have a tendency to gloss over any problems that don't support your gut feelings about what should be done.

Taking Action

We'd like you to consider three ideas when it comes to paying attention to process management tools and methods: study, devote, and embrace. First, **study** current processes to get a clear picture of what is and isn't working. Where is time and energy being wasted? If people are frustrated, why? Where does communication break down? Again, this means talking to people and slowing down to listen. The people in the trenches are often the ones with the best ideas because they spend time dwelling on these problems. If they offer solutions that don't fit into your current vision, consider carefully whether your vision may need to change. Next, realize that creating process changes is a lot of work. **Devote** enough time to do it right. Let people know what you're up to, and show them that it's a priority. Sometimes, very persistent inefficiencies may require moving backward before you can make progress forward, so prepare yourself mentally for some hard, seemingly thankless work. Finally, **embrace** your analytical side and do your homework to keep tabs on processes at regular intervals. Hone the skills that are relevant to process management in your field. For example, financial management skills are often a lot more useful in leadership than people realize. In any organization, finances impact many decisions. You'll also need to understand the work flow in your group, and you may need to fight your instincts to wing this or "guesstimate" it. You can't outsource a deep understanding of the processes that you oversee—you need to dig in and do the drudge work. This isn't to say that you can't get others involved, but you, as the leader, need to have a handle on exactly what your group is capable of and how you can use processes to reach better outcomes.

Conclusion

No matter where you fall on the leadership model, it's valuable to adopt some of the Deliberate leader's analytical, precise, and problem-solving ways, even if ever so slightly. Specifically, to be more Deliberate:

- Be deliberate in your communication,
- Show that you've done your homework, and
- Pay attention to process management tools and methods.

Case Study: Be Deliberate In Your Communication and Show That You've Done Your Homework

We spent some time talking to Ryan, a high-energy, sociable leader who has held posts as varied as executive chef and executive director, about his growth as a leader. In the past, Ryan went into staff meetings with a strong sense of what he wanted to convey, but he never wrote anything down and somewhere in the delivery, his message would get lost. As a result, people didn't always understand exactly what he wanted them to do. Because Ryan valued relationships, he didn't want to be seen as a micromanager. He wanted to be seen as a fun boss, and this often prevented him from creating enough structure or direction. "I want to just give my employees the steering wheel to the ship and let them go," he said, "but sometimes, what I really want them to do gets lost." At times, he doesn't explain things clearly enough, so Ryan has learned to be more deliberate about his communication. A few years ago, he got some interesting feedback from a fellow MBA student. "I had one person say to me, 'Man, Ryan, everyone always loves you in the group and responds to everything you say, and you present so well, but, there always seems to be nothing behind it.'" Ryan explained, "My personality doesn't [always reveal that] I've done the A, B, and C." Ryan learned that because he tends to make generalizations and focus on the big picture, people weren't always sure whether he'd done his homework. "The big picture—I'm so into that," he said. "And then when it gets down to the grunt work, it's like I have ADHD or something." Ryan has learned that through better organization and time management, he's able to create the discipline he needs to work out details and complete specific tasks that need to get done. This Energizing leader has found that by picking up a few suggestions from the Deliberate Dimension, he's a more effective leader.

Chapter 17

Lessons from Resolute Leaders

What Can We Learn from Resolute Leaders?

All leaders can learn a thing or two from the tough-minded ways of Resolute leaders. As we discussed in Chapter 2, the Resolute Dimension is located on the western side of the 8 Dimensions of Leadership Model, which means that Resolute leaders tend to be questioning and skeptical. In this chapter, we'll give you a clearer picture of the Resolute Dimension of leadership in real life.

Resolute leaders want to get efficient results, to ensure high quality outcomes, and to challenge themselves and others to do their best. They are matter-of-fact leaders who ask tough questions. When ideas don't seem solid, they push for more analysis. Resolute leaders tend to strike a balance between speed and quality, and both are quite important to them. They're both driven and analytical, though they're not quite as fast-paced as Commanding leaders nor as methodical as Deliberate leaders. Getting things right matters a great deal to Resolute leaders, and they may sometimes overlook the emotional aspects of leadership in their quest to accomplish their goals efficiently.

There are many benefits to the Resolute Dimension. Resolute leaders are willing to power through all kinds of garbage to reach the desired destination. Where many people would falter, they find a way. They welcome the challenge of solving a sticky problem, and they're not afraid of conflict if that's what it takes to reach a desirable outcome. When they see a red flag, they speak up, and they tend to confront such issues head-on. More than anything, they want to be seen as competent, and this often inspires them to perform their work both efficiently and conscientiously.

Strengths of Resolute Leaders

- They tend to be good problem solvers.
- They're often able to push their way through obstacles.
- They're able to hold people accountable.
- They're often able to identify potential weaknesses in plans.
- They're not afraid to speak their minds.
- They're usually able to separate feelings from issues.
- They have a competitive streak that helps them achieve their goals.
- They have high standards for themselves and others.

As you can see, there are many important leadership qualities that Resolute leaders have to offer to their organizations and to the world. Through years of leader-watching and research, we've developed three essential lessons that Resolute leaders have to offer. These three lessons are built around Resolute leaders' tendencies to be analytical and show great determination. If you think of yourself a Resolute leader, these lessons should validate your current leadership approach. Or, if you feel that your leadership could use a boost from the Resolute Dimension, use these three lessons and their complementary suggestions to strengthen your resolve.

Three Essential Lessons from Resolute Leaders

- Leaders need to have a fervent focus on outcomes.
- Tough problems that plague your team are your responsibility.
- The right decisions will upset people from time to time.

In this chapter, we'll explore these three lessons, dig into the obstacles that not-so-Resolute leaders might face, and offer suggestions for how to bring these lessons to life. Not all of the observations here will describe any one leader perfectly, but we think you'll gain some very useful insights into your fundamental assumptions and thought patterns around being Resolute.

Lesson One: Leaders Need to Have a Fervent Focus on Outcomes

Resolute leaders have an internal drive to push themselves. As a leader, not only is personal urgency important, but the ability to create a sense of urgency for a whole group—or even an organization—is vital at times. Resolute leaders often have a somewhat guarded posture toward others, and this enables them to show firmness when it comes to expectations. They don't just have high expectations for others, though—they expect a whole lot from themselves. They have a fighting spirit that serves them well when it comes to digging deep to drive toward their goals. Resolute leaders push for what they see as right. They aren't built to simply go with the flow. Admittedly, this might not always be a good recipe for happiness, but it no doubt leads to some impressive accomplishments.

Big Suggestion One: Learn to Hold People Accountable

Because many leaders can become overwhelmed with a desire to be admired or well liked, we'd like to promote the value of holding people accountable. Now, we're not suggesting that you overlook the human element entirely—far from it. Rather, we'd like to see you strike a healthy balance between people-orientation and task-orientation. As a leader, there are many ways to gain respect. People notice how you treat others, but they also care about the quality that you expect, the efficiency of your operations, and the bottom line. To be an effective leader, you need to cover your bases.

Is It Worth It?

In our research, we asked many leaders what career advice they would give themselves if they had it to do over again. One of the most consistently reported pieces of advice was to hold people more accountable. As one IT executive put it, he wishes he had "the moral courage to hold people accountable." Anything that takes moral courage certainly isn't easy! Holding people accountable tends to come more naturally to people with certain leadership styles than others. For example, many leaders whose styles fall on the eastern side of the model will struggle with this since they tend to be much more relationship-oriented than Resolute leaders. We've found that many experienced leaders report that they wish they would have learned this lesson sooner.

What are the benefits of learning to hold people accountable? Well, the obvious answer is that your group is more likely to meet its goals and deadlines if you take a firm stance. Not only that, but if you set high expectations for the group and then *don't* hold people accountable, you teach them that not pushing themselves is okay. Of course, part of the art of holding people accountable is setting challenging yet reasonable goals in the first place. If the goals aren't feasible, trying to hold people accountable will only lead to frustration and bad feelings. But, if the goals are appropriate, pushing the group to reach them can build camaraderie and increase people's feelings of self-worth. Finally, by holding *everyone* accountable, it creates an environment where people know what to expect.

Potential Obstacles to Holding People Accountable for Not-So-Resolute leaders

- You may have trouble seeing yourself as being in charge rather than just a part of the group.
- You may struggle to give direction without the group reaching consensus.
- You may harbor fears of coming across as demanding.
- You may lack the confidence to speak in an authoritative way.
- You may feel uncomfortable asking people to make sacrifices.
- You may have trouble separating your emotions from the task at hand.

Taking Action

Focus on three ideas when it comes to learning to hold people accountable: set, inquire, and analyze. First, **set** specific, aggressive, and concrete goals, and make sure that they are communicated to all involved. Better yet, involve others in setting the goals in the first place. Next, **inquire** about results on a regular basis. We're not advocating micromanagement. Rather, look at benchmarks to ensure that people are making adequate progress toward longer-term goals. Ask people where they're at and whether they need any support to get back on track. Don't wait until a deadline has come (and gone) to be surprised about delays. This is where balancing the Resolute leader's firm ways with some approachability could be very effective. If you expect people to come to you when they've hit roadblocks, you also need to be seen as approachable. Finally, when goals aren't met, **analyze** what went wrong. Avoid the temptation to just move on to the next goal. People need to learn that when things don't go as planned, attention will be paid and people will be held accountable. The problems will be uncovered and discussed so that the group can perform better in the future.

Lesson Two: Tough Problems That Plague Your Team Are Your Responsibility

Resolute leaders take responsibility for the tough—even ugly—problems that other leaders might want to ignore. Leaders have a responsibility to shore up organizational weaknesses, but many leaders—particularly those who thrive on optimism and enthusiasm—have a tendency to overlook this important part of leadership. In fact, leaders who aren't comfortable with conflict often gloss over problems rather than confront them head-on. Even if working out sticky issues is *not* what you find rewarding about leadership, there are times when it's vital.

Big Suggestion Two: Find and Address Problems

Many different types of leaders are conflict-averse, for various reasons. Some don't like things to get too emotional, while others just avoid anything that disrupts their equilibrium. The Resolute leader, on the other hand, has mastered how to *seek out* problems to fix. We're willing to bet that even when you try to avoid problems, you end up dealing with them down the road. This is a call for being more proactive about nipping problems in the bud. It may feel counterintuitive at first, but you may actually experience less conflict and stress by confronting issues sooner.

Is It Worth It?

As a leader, you are in a great position to increase the efficiency and effectiveness of your organization by fixing problems. Simply put, healthy organizations have healthy conflict. People don't sweep tensions under the rug, hoping that the issues won't resurface. Leaders don't let inefficiencies linger when there's a better way. When leaders step in and call attention to problems, they show others that the climate is safe to ask questions and suggest solutions. No doubt about it—halting the normal flow of work requires a great deal of energy. It requires overcoming the inertia of how things have always been done. If you make it clear that you don't want problems to slip through the cracks, others will probably step up to help you. And, believe it or not, by confronting issues upfront, you may actually experience less overall tension down the road. When issues are out in the open, everyone can get on board to help create solutions.

Potential Obstacles to Finding and Addressing Problems For Not-So-Resolute Leaders

- Your energy may be focused on the future, not on cleaning up the current state of affairs.
- You may be so focused on the positive that this simply feels unnatural.
- You may often hope for the best, assuming that problems will work themselves out.
- You may wait for solutions to come to you rather than seek them out.
- You may sometimes downplay the seriousness of problems to avoid having to get into something that could turn into a big deal.
- When confronted with a busy schedule, you may simply find it easier to tolerate a problem than to address it.

Taking Action

Focus on three things when it comes to finding and addressing problems: ask, weigh, and separate. Don't be afraid to **ask** others to help you identify problems and inefficiencies. This should be easy for leaders who are great with people, so get down in the trenches to see what people have to say about current methods. Try to understand things from their perspective, and make sure to ask a lot of questions. Don't be afraid to dig up some frustrations. Next, **weigh** the potential consequences of not addressing known issues in a timely manner. You may sometimes put off confronting a problem simply because you're not sure whether it's really a big deal. Carefully analyze the potential outcomes of both addressing the problem and of letting it simmer. Which poses a greater risk? When in doubt, ask a trusted colleague for some input. Finally, work to **separate** problems from people. Resolute leaders have learned that addressing problems doesn't have to be personal. In a leadership role, you will have to make changes that won't make everyone happy, and this can be hard on some leaders. Remind yourself that the goal of solving problems upfront is to make things better for everyone in the long run. With a sense of humor and some tact, you can bring up issues in a way that isn't hurtful.

Lesson Three: The Right Decisions Will Upset People from Time to Time

Resolute leaders are usually able to step back and make decisions objectively, and while they may (or may not) care what other people think, they don't feel the need to reach consensus before moving ahead. They recognize that not everyone is going to agree with their choices, and they set aside any personal considerations of wanting to be well liked in the interest of doing what they see as best for the organization. It's a little bit like parenting or teaching children—you can't always make decisions based on what they want. Sometimes, as the person in charge, you have a different perspective that allows you to see the big picture and make strategic choices that others might not understand. Resolute leaders are tough-minded people who aren't afraid to rock the boat with some unpopular decisions.

Big Suggestion Three: Get Comfortable Making Unpopular Decisions

Because many leaders, particularly those early in their careers, want to try to make everyone happy, we'd like to see you get comfortable making unpopular decisions. Resolute leaders can be tough-minded about separating out the emotional aspects from the decision-making process, but other leaders may struggle with this. When asked about his greatest strengths as a leader, one Resolute retail executive said, "the ability to manage with courage and make tough people decisions." It's interesting that he used the word "courage." It's not that Resolute leaders are entirely unfeeling. Rather, they're able to separate fact from emotion and prioritize their focus based on the situation at hand.

Is It Worth It?

Many leaders who have a high need for harmony struggle to make tough decisions, particularly when it comes to addressing entrenched, politically charged problems. Sam, an Affirming leader who serves as an elementary school principal, had to learn this lesson on the job. He said, "Sometimes, you have to deliver bad news or hold the line on a decision, or make a decision that you know 50% are going to be for and 50% are going to be against. You have to develop thicker skin very quickly and have to let go of the idea that you're going to be well liked." Many new leaders wrestle with the balance of wanting to be respected and well liked. We've all been frustrated at some point with politicians who make a decision that will get them re-elected rather than making the right long-term choice. As a leader, there are times when you need to acknowledge but move past people's objections. People often act from their own self interest (and that's normal), and it's sometimes your job to cut them off and not allow them to lead the group down the wrong path. Simply put, it's sometimes your job to be firm.

What are the benefits of getting comfortable with making unpopular decisions? At times, you'll face decisions that are clear-cut. Few people will disagree with your choice, and things will head smoothly in the new direction. Hopefully that happens quite regularly! However, there will be stickier situations in which choosing one direction leads to seemingly negative consequences for certain groups of people. If you've done your homework and determined that the unpopular decision is the one that will help your organization reach its goals, you need to have the resolve to act. Explaining your decision carefully and clearly may go a long way to help people see where you're coming from, but there will always be some who don't get on board, and that's okay. The bottom line is that you're acting in the best interest of the organization, and this is your job as a leader. Making less-than-optimal decisions just to avoid rocking the boat can lead to inefficiencies, mistakes, and missed opportunities.

Potential Obstacles to Making Unpopular Decisions for Not-So-Resolute Leaders

- You may not like the idea of inconveniencing people.
- You may find it difficult to take a stand on issues that are political in nature.
- You may have strong instincts to stay in your comfort zone.
- You may find it uncomfortable to act against dissenting opinions of people you like and respect.
- You may be tempted to soften up your message to make it easier to swallow.
- You may have a hard time accepting that people might complain about you and your decisions.

Taking Action

Focus on three ideas when it comes to learning to make unpopular decisions: seek, take, and connect. First, **seek** multiple sources of data when you need to make major decision. Do include other people's opinions as part of your data collection, but also look at how each choice fits with your big-picture vision and whether the specifics add up. Next, **take** a proactive stance about announcing your decisions. Don't procrastinate or let the information leak out in bits and pieces. If you feel good about your decision and see it as a win for the organization, sell it that way. Finally, **connect** the dots for people. Carefully explain the benefits of the decision, back it up with data if relevant, and then give people a chance to react. Expect that some people won't be on board, but keep in mind that many people have trouble with anything that shakes up the status quo. We're not suggesting that you should be entirely closed-off to negative feedback, but to a certain extent, you need to channel your leadership energy forward. Acknowledge objections but help people move toward the goal.

Conclusion

Whatever your primary leadership dimension, it's valuable to adopt some of the Resolute leader's questioning, matter-of-fact, and determined ways, even if ever so slightly. Specifically, to be more Resolute:

- Learn to hold people accountable,
- Find and address problems, and
- Get comfortable making unpopular decisions.

Case Study: Get Comfortable Making Unpopular Decisions

We talked more with Sam, an elementary school principal, about making tough decisions. "It's clear that in a school there are certain interest groups," he said, "and [tough decisions could include] designing a schedule that benefits the kindergarten and 1st grade teachers but puts a burden on the 4th and 5th grade teachers' ability to do their job. It might be a certain way that you do your building dismissal that really helps out the teachers, but it's hard on the specialists." Throw parents and students into the mix, and making decisions that please everyone seems almost impossible. He talked about the tension between wanting to be well liked but also to be respected—something that is naturally hard for an Inclusive leader like Sam. For him, it was helpful to realize that it's just part of the job. "You're watching your colleagues, and you're watching how other principals work through this, and you do have to distance yourself a little bit," he said. "You're not going to be able to attend the staff functions in the same way because you are making those decisions and you're making staff and personnel decisions. So you do distance yourself a little bit and your relationships are not as personal as they would be with the teaching team, if you were a teacher on that team. I think the other piece, too, is when you have either a mentor or a colleague group that you can commiserate with and collaborate with, you find out that these are very common occurrences, and so you realize that you're really filling a role and not wrecking people's lives with your decisions."

Chapter 18

Lessons from Commanding Leaders

What Can We Learn from Commanding Leaders?

We all can learn some valuable leadership lessons from the Commanding leaders among us who bring so much ambition and intensity to their work. As we discussed in Chapter 2, the Commanding Dimension is located in the northwestern area of the 8 Dimensions of Leadership Model, which means that Commanding leaders tend to be fast-paced and outspoken, as well as questioning and skeptical. This adds up to a person who's hard-charging and driven. In this chapter, we'll help you understand why these people so frequently find themselves in leadership positions and what you can borrow from them.

Commanding leaders want to blaze a trail toward their goals, to have their vision realized, and more than anything, to win. They love nothing more than to cross the finish line and see the looks on people's faces. Ah, the thrill of victory! They often take on the world, shouldering responsibility for anything and everything they can get their hands on. They pour tremendous amounts of energy into their work, and nothing gives Commanding leaders more satisfaction than clearing a path through obstacles, doubt, and resistance.

The benefits to this style of leadership are numerous. Leaders who are high on the Commanding Dimension are quick thinkers who are often comfortable making on-the-fly decisions based on their gut instincts. They tend to be confident, and they don't like to watch from the sidelines. In fact, being forced to take the backseat, particularly in a crisis, feels like torture to Commanding leaders. They aren't afraid to push ahead, even in situations in which they fall short on experience or expertise. When faced with a task, they want to execute immediately, and they may create shortcuts to move things along more aggressively. Finally, they tend to see themselves as realists. They pride themselves on having a strong backbone, and they expect this type of fortitude from others.

Strengths of Commanding Leaders

- They're able to set and stick to aggressive timelines.
- They tend to be very goal-oriented.
- They're able to speak with conviction.
- They're not afraid to take some risks.
- They're comfortable stepping up to take charge when a group lacks direction.
- They're able to make tough decisions that may not be popular.
- They set high expectations for themselves and others.

Commanding leaders have so many gifts to offer, both to their organizations and to the world. Based on extensive research, we've developed three essential lessons that we can all learn from Commanding leaders. These three lessons are built around Commanding leaders' tendencies to be forceful, direct, and driven. If you see yourself as a Commanding leader, these lessons should make you feel good about your current leadership approach. Or, if you strive to develop a more Commanding presence, use these three lessons and suggestions to dial up this dimension.

Three Essential Lessons from Commanding Leaders

- Personal authority matters.
- Getting caught up in unnecessary restrictions can dilute leadership effectiveness.
- Impatience can be a virtue.

In this chapter, we'll explore these three lessons, point out some obstacles that not-so-Commanding leaders might face, and offer suggestions for how to bring these lessons to life. Not all of the observations here will describe any one leader perfectly, but we think you'll gain some very useful insights into your fundamental assumptions and thought patterns around being Commanding.

Lesson One: Personal Authority Matters

Commanding leaders often serve as a rock from which others draw confidence and direction. Many leaders who are relatively low on the Commanding Dimension—especially those who are early on in their careers—have tendencies that prevent them from exercising their personal authority. They may simply be uncomfortable with power, so they often downplay their own status, preferring to defer to others they see as more charismatic or authoritative. Subconsciously, these leaders may associate power with somehow doing people harm, so they often want to give away power. In fact, leaders who aren't comfortable with personal authority sometimes try to make themselves as inconspicuous as possible.

Big Suggestion One: Get Comfortable Making Firm, Public Commitments

When leaders who are low on the Commanding Dimension avoid making public commitments, they are seen as weak, ineffective, or perhaps submissive. Organizations require commitment and consistency from leaders to shape ongoing decisions and actions. Some leaders who rely on consensus and risk mitigation struggle with doubts about being "wrong." Therefore, it's natural that these leaders—often those whose styles fall in the eastern and southern areas of the model—may need more practice in exercising their personal authority.

Is It Worth It?

Leaders who tend to filter their messages to accommodate others may not realize how much more efficient it would be just to tell people what they really think. Firmness suggests confidence, and people instinctively trust that a firm leader understands something important. When Commanding leaders speak firmly, people often see them as more discerning and critical, and this may give more credibility to their ideas. Now, you may have an aversion to the idea of *being critical,* but there is tremendous value in discernment when it comes to leadership (We talk more about this in the Deliberate Dimension). Consider the role of critics. Whether critics review books, movies, or restaurants, their task is the same—to discern the good from the mediocre, to steer people toward that which is worthy of their time and money. A critic who gives every review an A+ or five stars provides little value, and the same can be said for leaders who aren't willing to state honest, specific opinions.

As we've discussed, leaders are responsible for initiating change, and this requires a show of power. For a major initiative to get off the ground, someone needs to stand up and confidently say, "We're going to do this!" Let's imagine the alternative. What would happen if a bunch of people thought something was a good idea, but no one stood up and took charge? Absolutely nothing. Or worse: chaos. Leaders who are low on the Commanding Dimension are often tempted to leave taking charge to those who they see as above them, but this severely limits their potential as leaders.

Genevra, a senior product manager at a manufacturing and consumer goods company, told us that she had to grow into her new leadership role, particularly with regard to personal authority. Advice she'd like to give others who are not-so-Commanding by nature includes, "Work on being less shy and more self-confident." Leadership means helping people see how to get from here to there—*there* being the vision you have for the future. By learning how to show more personal authority, you'll be better able to mobilize people to work toward mutual goals.

Potential Obstacles to Getting Comfortable with Power for Not-So-Commanding Leaders

- You may have trouble thinking of yourself as powerful—particularly if it means having power over other people.

- You may have an impulse to give the power to someone else or to share it.

- You may prefer to blend into the crowd.

- You may have a lot of uncertainty about your ability to divine the truth on your own.

- You may hate the idea of making decisions that might misguide others.

- You may think of taking charge as a little harsh because you worry about negatively impacting others.

Taking Action

Consider three ideas when it comes to making firm, public commitments: believe, practice, and monitor. First, learn to **believe** that you are genuinely powerful and capable of making firm decisions. It will make the job of leading much, much less stressful, and all of the mental energy that you pour into doubt can be used for more productive purposes. Research suggests that people who are simply made to feel powerful are much more likely to act quickly and take action, perhaps because they see the environment as less dangerous (Gollwitzer et al, 1990). Second, **practice** exercising your personal power by standing firmly behind your decisions. Start in a setting in which you're relatively comfortable, and go from there. At first, it may feel like throwing yourself out of a plane, not knowing if the parachute is going to work, but if you don't *feel* very powerful, it sometimes helps simply to *pretend* that you are. Finally, start to **monitor** the voice in your head that tells you *not* to think of yourself as powerful. If you call attention to these feelings when you recognize them, they will gradually lose their power over you.

Lesson Two: Getting Caught Up In Unnecessary Restrictions Can Dilute Leadership Effectiveness

Commanding leaders have the confidence to act decisively, and leaders who struggle in this area can gain some inspiration from their ability to act. In our research, the number one thing that leaders were asked to do more of was to find new opportunities—something that many leaders whose styles fall on the northern side of the model enjoy. Why is this? Well, if leaders don't see things in a new light—don't wonder what could be—their groups aren't likely to evolve. There are some people in your organization who no doubt have a preference for peace over stimulation, but there are many who want to push toward bigger and better. When leaders put unnecessary restrictions on themselves, it can keep them not only from finding new opportunities, but from actually having the courage to act on them.

Big Suggestion Two: Learn to Act without Permission Let go of—stomp on—some of the assumed limitations that are holding you back. When you find yourself saying that something can't or shouldn't be done, catch yourself. Put aside the "can't" momentarily and ask yourself whether it would be worth it if you could work around the problem. If you put your mind to it, there's often a way to work around the supposed rules. We're not talking about breaking laws or bending your ethics; we're talking about the rules that you impose on yourself to maintain a sense of security. How can you start to see them less as being set in stone and more as temporary roadblocks? Early in her career, a leader named Carol—now president of a large division of an international publisher—realized that her job would be a lot easier if she weren't running back and forth from her office to the fax machine. At the time, her company had a policy against fax machines in individuals' offices. Carol had the good sense to realize that this rule was hindering her leadership effectiveness, so she challenged it and took charge. Looking back, she wishes she had learned to take control sooner. Sure, it's important to respect the hierarchy and your place in it, but we're asking you to learn to act without permission when the situation calls for it.

Is It Worth It?

Let's explore the benefits of learning to act without permission. One study on power involved placing participants in a room with an annoying fan pointed at them (Galinsky et al, 2003). The researchers found that when participants were asked to write about a time when they had power over someone, they were more likely to take action with regards to the fan. On the other hand, when participants were asked to write about a time when someone had power over *them*, they were significantly less likely to move the fan or turn it off. When leaders see themselves as powerful, they allow themselves to shift things as they see fit. They make the rules. They don't see others as more powerful than they are, nor more entitled to have a say.

What are the benefits of acting without permission? Many times, other people look to leaders to take the first step or to speak up when there's a problem. When you consistently defer your personal power to other people—and even to circumstances—you send the message that you have little control over your environment. Not only do you send this message to others, but you send it to yourself. If you hope to align people around your vision for the future, it's important that both you and others see you as someone who has personal power. We're not talking about being a bully or an egomaniac. We're talking about giving yourself permission to take action and take charge.

Potential Obstacles to Acting Without Permission for Not-So-Commanding Leaders

- You may not be comfortable wielding the assertiveness, if not aggressiveness, required to take charge.
- It may be difficult for you to overcome inertia in order to act.
- You may have strong instincts to stay on the safe path.
- You may struggle to leave your comfort zone.
- You may hate to "bother" people with your ideas.
- You may prefer to avoid the possibility of upsetting others and their routines.

Taking Action

Consider three ideas when it comes to learning to act without permission: brainstorm, control, and rewrite. First, set aside time to **brainstorm** what's possible, and *think big*. Think about what the group or organization *really* needs, rather than what others have decided that it needs. *You* are creating a vision for the future—take the opportunity to imagine what could be. Push aside thoughts of restrictions, rules, and roadblocks, and be decisive! Next, don't be afraid to be the one to take **control** of situations in which a group seems to be floundering, either through inactivity, discord, or chaos. Someone needs to step up to guide the group toward a solution, and that someone can be you! Be proactive about bringing people together to solve problems. State what you see happening, and ask people to offer solutions. Finally, if current "rules" are no longer relevant, give yourself permission to **rewrite** the rules. We're not talking about laws—

we're talking about the way things are done in your organization. Step back periodically to look at the big picture. If certain rules and restrictions seem to be standing in the way of progress—and other people may bring these to your attention—take an honest look at what's going on. Don't be afraid to rewrite the rules.

Lesson Three: Impatience Can Be a Virtue

Commanding leaders are able to push the group to work beyond what's comfortable to get results. This involves both initiating action and helping the group maintain momentum. Leaders who are lower on the Commanding Dimension have several tendencies that may cause them to fall short on this at times. Some may simply prefer a more steady, comfortable pace. They don't like to feel rushed—they'd rather take the time to get things done right. If you consider the 8 Dimensions of Leadership Model, this makes a lot of sense. Remember that those styles on the southern side of the model tend to be cautious and reflective, while those on the northern side—such as the Commanding Dimension—are fast-paced and outspoken. Leaders who are more cautious tend to process all of the information before acting, and this can cause them to be less responsive to changing environments. When every adjustment of the rudder requires lengthy deliberation, the organization becomes less nimble and innovative.

Big Suggestion Three: Create Some Urgency

Commanding leaders have a way of creating a sense of urgency—a subtle or not-so-subtle pressure—that keeps the group pushing toward results. As a leader, you need to strike a delicate balance between creating a highly functioning, secure environment and creating this type of pressure to keep moving, sometimes at breathtaking speed. We're not saying that the pressure has to be negative. There are many ways to create a sense of urgency, and we'll try to help you find ways to do this that complement your personality. For example, urgency can come in the form of generating excitement about a goal. Leaders can inspire people to want to achieve a goal quickly so they can move onto even more exciting opportunities.

Is It Worth It?

Let's explore the benefits of creating some urgency. As a leader, you have a responsibility to set the tone for the group. No doubt about it—you probably already do some important things to create a positive atmosphere. Leaders who are lower on the Commanding Dimension are often good at helping everyone feel comfortable, but there's a danger in letting people get too comfortable. If you don't show some energy, people tend to plod along at a comfortable pace and focus more on their individual comfort than on the group's goals. Not only does this delay progress, but it can kill the motivation of people in your group who may actually prefer to work at a faster pace.

As a leader, you can help shape people's goals and motivations. When leaders show urgency and excitement, people adjust to the expectations. When deadlines are firm and schedules are tight, people rise to the occasion and accomplish more than they even knew they could. Think about it—by pushing people, you can help them become more effective as individuals. And by minimizing inefficiencies and cutting out unnecessary processes, you can help everyone accomplish more together. Creating some urgency can have some very positive effects on your organization's bottom line *and* its morale.

Potential Obstacles to Creating Some Urgency for Not-So-Commanding Leaders

- You may prefer to work at a more methodical pace to ensure accuracy.
- You may often have a sense that things will "happen when they happen."
- Pressuring people may feel incredibly uncomfortable to you.

- You may not see yourself as capable of commanding people's attention.
- You may get so caught up in thinking about what could go wrong that it's difficult to sell your plans to others.

Taking Action

Focus on three ideas when it comes to creating some urgency: enlist, show, and hold. Start creating a sense of urgency by making it a collaborative effort. **Enlist** other people. Ask them to help you set more aggressive schedules. By including them in the process, they're much more likely to feel invested. Next, **show** some excitement about the potential outcomes, and help people see how they fit into the big picture of the goals. Explain why the urgency is needed. Because the leader often sets the pace for the group, you'll need to lead by example. Finally, **hold** people accountable. Put your expectations into writing, reiterate deadlines, and check in with people to see how they're progressing. If someone falls short, avoid the temptation to shrug it off. You'll both learn more if you can engage them in a thoughtful dialogue about what went wrong. We think you can be successful at creating a sense of urgency while being true to your values as a leader. There's no need to feel uncomfortable about helping a group gain and maintain momentum.

Conclusion

Whatever your primary approach to leadership, it's valuable to adopt some of the Commanding leader's driven, forceful, and dominant ways, even if ever so slightly. Specifically, to be more Commanding:

- Get comfortable making firm, public commitments,
- Learn to act without permission, and
- Create some urgency.

Case Study: Learn to Act Without Permission

We talked more with Carol, the president of a division of an international publishing company, about how she learned to avoid getting caught up in unnecessary restrictions. "When I became a general manager—this is actually just a very practical thing that [a colleague] told me—and this will sound really tactical," she said, "but I've interpreted it more broadly. He said, 'the most important thing a general manager needs is a fax in the office.'" At the time, she was involved in dividing an organization and allocating resources. Between important phone calls, she was running to the fax or the printer to grab confidential documents before anyone else saw them. "A few times," she said, "other people accidentally picked them up with their big printing jobs." Based on this experience, Carol saw the value in learning to act without permission. "What I've become convinced of is if there's something I really need to do my job, then it doesn't matter if there's the formal policy that you're not supposed to have printers in your office," she said, "or don't worry about spending $200 if it's going to help me do a better job for the company. I still am very thrifty, but there have been times when I just remember that [experience]." She added that this lesson applies to more than just printers or faxes. It's more about allowing yourself to act without permission to maximize efficiency, get better results, or jump on a new opportunity.

Chapter 19

Pulling it all Together

Leadership is a uniquely complex undertaking, no matter if the group being led is a nonprofit organization, a Fortune 500 company, or a jazz trio. Some organizations make leadership development a core discipline because it is critical to the well-being of the organization and sometimes even to the safety of its members. Unfortunately, for the vast majority of group endeavors, leadership is expected, but there is no rigorous method and few resources directed toward developing people to function in leadership roles.

Peter Drucker (1996) observed that in many respects, effective leaders behave in much the same way: They begin by asking, "What needs to be done?" and then they ask, "What can and should I do to make a difference?" Our goal for readers of *The 8 Dimensions of Leadership* is to give you a flexible framework to help you answer these two questions and to begin expanding your capacity to inspire, energize, support, analyze, and direct those who are relying on you to make a difference.

Many successful leaders reflect on their development and note that there were no signs, no instruction manual, and very little opportunity for practice rounds. The lessons in *The 8 Dimensions of Leadership* are designed to give you specific advice around new approaches to exercising your responsibilities as a leader. Now it's up to *you* to decide how far you want to go in strengthening those dimensions that don't come naturally to you. All of the lessons and suggestions we describe here are in the behavioral repertoire of people at every level of any organization. You get to choose where to focus your energy. We suggest that over time, you work to increase your capacity across all of the dimensions. Chances are that you will be called upon to demonstrate each of the dimensions somewhere in the course of your career.

The Value in Multiple Leadership Dimensions

The need for diversity of leadership behaviors is simply too often overlooked. A number of people reviewing our work have asked if there is bias in the model because the "more favorable" leadership characteristics are located on the northern side of our model (Commanding, Pioneering, Energizing). Our answer is that most readers actually have *more* to learn from the southern dimensions (Deliberate, Humble, Inclusive), and that though different, these are equally valuable.

We are not the first to assert that there is more to leadership than charisma. In his 2001 book, *Good to Great: Why Some Companies Make the Leap…and Others Don't*, Jim Collins noted that one of the most surprising findings in his research study was that a very specific style of leadership—"Level 5 Leadership"—made a profound difference in turning good organizations into great ones. The characteristics of Level 5 Leadership have remarkable alignment with the dimensions located on our model—including the southern side. According to Collins, "Level 5 leaders embody a paradoxical mix of personal humility and professional will" (p 39). His research team was not looking for leadership to be a major factor in successful companies, but the data were compelling—Level 5 leadership was a consistent differentiator of "great" companies. "The great irony is that the animus and personal ambition that often drive people to positions of power stand at odds with the humility required for Level 5 leadership," (36) he writes. We don't think there is a better argument for the benefits of developing flexibility around all eight dimensions of our leadership model.

We believe that multidimensionality of leadership styles applies not only to individuals, but to organizations as well. Imagine the culture of an organization where all managerial and executive ranks are filled by inflexible, Commanding leaders. Imagine the single-minded focus on winning, the potential for group think, the potential for unmitigated risk-taking—but enough about Wall Street circa 2008. We suspect that organizations that value a wide array of leadership styles will, in the long run, outperform those that systematically favor a single leadership dimension. The lessons associated with each of the eight leadership dimensions can serve as a useful vocabulary to understand competencies that are present or absent in your organization's culture. Although we have yet to study the 8 Dimensions among groups, we suspect that the greater the diversity of approaches in an organization, the better.

Moving Forward

It's clear that great leadership requires a balance of characteristics, many of which are seemingly at odds. The idea of mastering all eight dimensions is probably overwhelming, but we're not asking you to do that today. As you prepare to work on some of the dimensions that are less natural for you, it may be helpful to organize your thoughts on which lessons and suggestions you found *most* valuable in Part 3. We summarize the suggestions here to help you reflect on where you want to focus your energy now:

To Be More Pioneering

- ☐ Actively seek new opportunities beyond your organization's walls.
- ☐ Break some glass.
- ☐ Learn to take leaps of faith.

To Be More Energizing

- ☐ Make an effort to build enthusiasm for the group's goals.
- ☐ Be intentional about making connections with a wide variety of people.
- ☐ Learn to lead the rally.

To Be More Affirming

- ☐ Monitor your "default" expressions.
- ☐ Let people know that you value them.
- ☐ Accept other people's limitations.

To Be More Inclusive

- ☐ Show people that you're open to their ideas.
- ☐ Monitor your emotional output carefully.
- ☐ Work to facilitate two-way discussion on important issues.

To Be More Humble

- ☐ Maintain your composure by keeping things in perspective.
- ☐ Take the time to listen to the less powerful people around you.
- ☐ Make the needs of your group a priority.

To Be More Deliberate

- ☐ Be deliberate in your communication.
- ☐ Show that you've done your homework.
- ☐ Pay attention to process management tools and methods.

To Be More Resolute

- ☐ Learn to hold people accountable.
- ☐ Find and address problems.
- ☐ Get comfortable making unpopular decisions.

To Be More Commanding

☐ Get comfortable with making firm, public commitments.

☐ Learn to act without permission.

☐ Create some urgency.

Now that you've prioritized what you want to work on, take some time to consider how you best implement change. Some people need to put their goals in writing, others prefer to share their intentions with a friend, and some like to have a mentor or coach who can provide support along the way. What works best for you? As you think about how to implement the lessons, here are some things to consider:

- Would it be helpful to get feedback from others on what you most need to work on, either informally or through a 360° assessment process?

- Who can serve as a role model or mentor to you in one or more of these areas?

- How will you hold yourself accountable for the growth you hope to achieve?

- What are some potential barriers that you might face?

- How will you know whether you've been successful?

As you move forward, remember that the 8 Dimensions of Leadership Model is dynamic. Your primary leadership dimension does not confine you to one place on the model, and your knowledge of all eight dimensions should provide you with a new sense of possibility. There are some valid alternatives to your current leadership style, some of which may be exactly what others have been hoping to see from you. Once you have selected the lessons you want to work on and have created the structure to help you achieve your goals, it's time to practice, practice, practice. Again—the goal is to lead like you, only better.

Appendix

DiSC® Background, Theory, and Research

Although the DiSC® model was developed almost a century ago, DiSC research became much more focused and systematic in the 1970s. Since that time, the heart of the model has remained the same, but our current understanding of DiSC is far more advanced. Our third generation of DiSC reflects not only advancements in the general field of psychology, but also a forty-year program of research into the model. In this appendix, we want to give you a brief description of the core concepts behind DiSC and explain, both conceptually and empirically, how this theory was used to develop the 8 Dimensions of Leadership Model.

The Basics behind the DiSC Model

The Two DiSC Axes

There are two basic axes that serve as the foundation of DiSC. As you can see in Figure A.1, the horizontal and vertical axes create quadrants that are the D, i, S, and C styles. Understanding these two axes is the key to recognizing the relationships among the

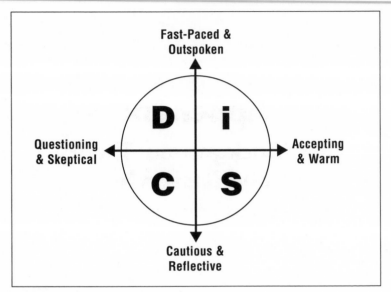

Figure A.1. The DiSC Axes

styles and applying the model in a real world setting. Chapter 2 describes how these play out in the domain of leadership. Here we will look at the axes from a more technical and historical perspective.

The vertical axis runs from fast-paced and outspoken to cautious and reflective. It describes one's outward activity level and assertiveness. Traditionally, those at the northern end of the axis (i.e., the D and i styles) were described as "seeing themselves as more powerful than the environment." As a consequence, they were more likely to be bold and project confidence. Those at the southern end of the axis (i.e., the S and C styles) were traditionally described as "seeing themselves as less powerful than the environment." Therefore, they were more likely to adapt to current circumstances and work within existing parameters. At times, they have been referred to as "passive," but the connotations of this label distract from the strengths that these two styles bring to an organization.

The horizontal axis has been the source of much more confusion over the years. After a full year of research on this specific issue, we concluded that this axis is best described as running from questioning and skeptical to accepting and warm. Those on the western side of the model (i.e., the D and C styles) were traditionally described as "perceiving the environment as antagonistic to their interests." That is, they are more likely to view the world as resistant or unwelcoming to their needs. As a consequence, these people tend to be skeptical of new people or ideas, not always trusting information at face value. Our newest research suggests that people with a combined DC style frequently describe themselves as questioning or challenging.

Those on the eastern side of the model (i.e., the i and S styles) were traditionally described as "perceiving the environment as aligned with their interests." That is, they trust their environment. New information or new people are likely to be accepted at face value. People with a combined iS style tend to describe themselves as cheerful, caring, and receptive.

It is worth noting that the horizontal axis of DiSC is sometimes described as being a task-oriented vs. people-oriented axis. Our research continually refutes this. We find that many people with the S style describe themselves as task-oriented and many people with the D style describe themselves as people-oriented. The task-people axis more correctly appears to run diagonally from the C style to the i style.

The Four Styles

The four quadrants of the DiSC map have been labeled Dominance, Influence, Steadiness (originally Submissiveness), and Conscientiousness (originally Compliance). The four styles are described as follows:

Dominance: describes people who are driven and forceful. They usually have strong opinions about how things should be done and are direct, if not blunt, with those opinions. They often describe themselves as aggressive, strong-willed, and demanding.

Influence: describes people who are enthusiastic and high-spirited. They're quick to seek out new social opportunities and are generally very talkative. This style combines a high level of energy with a strong positive disposition.

Steadiness: describes people who are gentle and accommodating. They're very considerate of other people's needs and show a great deal of patience. They work to create an environment around them that is stable and harmonious.

Conscientiousness: describes people who are analytical and reserved. They place a high value on accuracy and take a systematic approach to their work. Emotional displays are kept to a minimum, as they put a strong emphasis on logic and reason.

DiSC as a Circumplex

The four DiSC styles are, in essence, a typology. They are categories that help us quickly understand individual differences. Although a person is often said to have one particular style, it is important to recognize that most people can stretch into all of these areas when the situational demands are pressing enough. In fact, the parsing of the model into four quadrants is, from a theoretical perspective, arbitrary. It could just as easily have been divided into eight sections or twelve sections (although four styles are much easier for the average person to remember than eight or twelve). The point is, the four styles should not be viewed as discrete, unrelated categories. We are all a blend of the four styles, but tend to favor some more than others.

When William Marston initially presented the DiSC model, he compared it to the color wheel in which each of the colors blends gently into adjacent colors. Our research confirms that this is a very apt analogy and that DiSC can accurately be described as a *circumplex*. As a technical designation, DiSC's circumplex structure has a host of mathematical implications for the theory. But in lay terms, "circumplex" means that all areas of the DiSC model are equally valid and meaningful. One person may have a pure D style, while another person has a mostly D style with a slight leaning toward the C style. One style blends into an adjacent style much the same way red blends into orange. As we will see momentarily, this insight allows for some profound improvements in the measurement and application of the model.

The Measurement of DiSC

John Geier was one of the early researchers to build a formal measurement system to Marston's concepts. His tool assigned scores to the test taker on each of the four styles and presented these scores in the form of a line graph. The styles were treated like separate domains, largely independent from each other. In the early 1970s, the DiSC model and instrument was first commercialized in the business community by Geier's company, which later became Inscape Publishing.

Although research on the DiSC model persisted through the '80s and '90s, the presentation of DiSC as a pure typology remained the same. A second generation of DiSC measurement developed at Inscape by Pamela Cole and Gary Little took advantage of computerized assessment and offered test takers personalized narrative to accompany their D, i, S, and C scores. By the early 2000s, however, a deeper insight into both DiSC theory and psychometric theory allowed for a third generation of the model in which DiSC was measured as a circumplex. Not only is this conceptualizing of DiSC more consistent with Marston's original writing, but it is also much more representative of developments in contemporary academic psychology (e.g., the interpersonal circle.)

Instead of measuring and presenting DiSC as four discrete scales, DiSC was measured as eight intercorrelated scales equally spaced around the DiSC circle. Not only were D, i, S, and C measured, but blends of the styles were also measured (i.e., Di, iS, SC, and CD). From these eight scales, an individual could be located on the two DiSC axes and then plotted within the DiSC circumplex, as shown in Figure A.2. Beyond being more

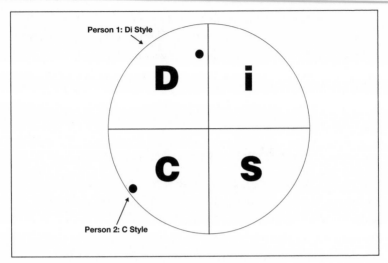

Figure A.2. Example of DiSC circumplex results

conceptually accurate, this method of presenting results has a host of other advantages. For instance, two individuals could much more easily visualize their similarities and differences within the DiSC model. Or, a lone individual could more easily visualize the effort required to stretch from, let's say, the C style to the i style.

The research was exceptionally supportive of this new method of measuring DiSC. New data continues to support both the validity and reliability of the assessment. For instance, scientists look at the "internal reliability" of a scale to assess if that scale is measuring a single unified concept. A metric called "Cronbach's Alpha" is used to evaluate internal reliability. This metric ranges from 0 to 1 and is expected to be above .70 for a given scale before being considered acceptable. As shown in the diagonal of Table A.1, each of the DiSC scales well exceeds this value. Table A.1 also shows the intercorrelations among the DiSC scales. As expected under circumplex theory, adjacent scales (e.g., the S and Si scales) are most highly correlated and scales opposite each other on the DiSC model (e.g., the S and D scales) have a strong negative correlation.

	D	Di	i	iS	S	SC	C	CD
D	**.88**							
Di	.37	**.91**						
i	-.04	.51	**.91**					
iS	-.49	-.10	.38	**.88**				
S	-.71	-.42	-.05	.49	**.82**			
SC	-.52	-.75	-.63	-.11	.37	**.82**		
C	-.05	-.55	-.76	-.44	-.06	.54	**.80**	
CD	-.35	-.18	-.50	-.69	-.51	.15	.39	**.75**

Bold numbers across the diagonal represent coefficient Alphas for the eight DiSC scales.

Table A.1. DiSC Scales Intercorrelations and Reliabilities

The Application of the DiSC Circumplex

Although not necessarily called "DiSC," the fundamental concepts behind DiSC are continually rediscovered by thinkers and researchers in a wide variety of disciplines. In academic psychology, the DiSC concepts are referred to as the "interpersonal circle." In Ancient Greece, Hippocrates referred to them as the "four humours." The reason that this model continues to pop up again and again is because DiSC addresses very fundamental aspects of human nature that have a profound impact on how we do our work and how we relate to each other.

DiSC is a general measure of personality, but it has long been applied to a variety of professional domains. An individual with a particular style is thought to have specific priorities on the job and gravitate toward certain job-relevant behaviors. Before expanding the DiSC circumplex into the field of leadership, we began researching two professional fields that have long used the DiSC model to help develop workers: management and sales.

We expected that tasks and attitudes of managers and salespeople would take a shape that closely resembled the DiSC circumplex. For example, we asked managers what is important to them on the job and were able to plot out their preferences in two-dimensional space using a technique called multidimensional scaling. What we found was that the managers' attitudes conformed quite remarkably to the basic DiSC model. Take a look at Figure A.3. Each dot represents a management priority, and the closer two dots are to one another, the more

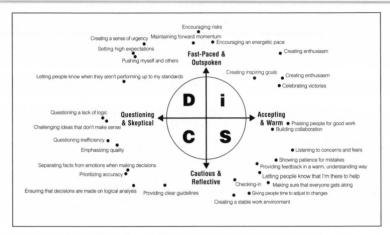

Figure A.3. Multidimensional plotting of management priorities

similar they are. So, managers who cared about "creating a sense of urgency" were also likely to care about "setting high expectations," but less likely to care about "providing feedback in a warm, understanding way." It's easy to see how management priorities clearly reflect the DiSC circumplex.

We conducted similar studies in the area of sales. In one such study, salespeople were presented with fourteen sales tasks relating to customer interactions and asked to rate how important each was when they were interacting with clients. The results, as shown in Figure A.4, clearly show the relevance of

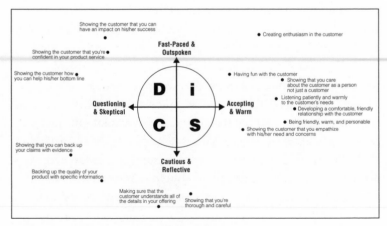

Figure A.4. Multidimensional plotting of sales tasks

the DiSC model. For example, the tasks in the upper left-hand corner reflect a results orientation, which is typical of the D style, and the task in the lower left-hand corner reflect a priority on quality and evidence, which is typical of the C style.

This research supports what DiSC practitioners have been teaching for years: DiSC, as a measure of personality, helps explain how people approach their jobs in a variety of different professional fields.

The Application of DiSC to Leadership

We began our investigation by reviewing the work of contemporary and traditional thought leaders in the leadership arena. Additionally, we reviewed academic research in the field to help differentiate between the supported and unsupported theories and assertions. We found that DiSC had a great deal to say about the interpersonal concepts that were being discussed by thought leaders such as Jack Zenger, Peter Drucker, John Kotter, Jim Kouzes and Barry Posner, Sun Tzu, Jack Welch, Robert Greenleaf, Warren Bennis, Edgar Schein, Stephen Covey, Larry Bossidy and Ram Charan, Daniel Goleman, Peter Senge, and Jim Collins.

After identifying the leadership constructs that were relevant to the DiSC model, we began the data collection stage of the project. In twelve rounds of data collection, 26,899 participants were asked questions about their own leadership performances as well as the performances of leaders in their previous or current organizations. These data were used to identify and build initial leadership scales and understand the psychometric relationships among various leadership constructs.

Next, leaders were chosen from a wide range of industries. For these leaders, managers, peers, direct reports, and other colleagues were selected to rate the leaders' performance on the initial leadership scales. Leaders were also asked to rate their own performance. Based on these results, the leadership scales were refined. More importantly, however, we began to see the emergence of a very clear leadership model that explained the relationship among these leadership constructs. This, of course, was to become the 8 Dimensions of Leadership Model.

After this model development stage, we conducted research with over 3000 additional raters to confirm the validity of this model. These studies confirmed both the ability to measure the proposed leadership constructs and the robustness of the leadership model. If you look at Table A.2, you can see the eight dimension scales, along with three subscales that fall under each. The Alpha values in the second column suggest exceptional reliability for each of these scales.

Additionally, the correlations among the scales offered strong support for the 8 Dimensions of Leadership Model. Figure A.5 offers a visual representation of the relationships among the scales using multidimensional scaling (MDS). (Keep in mind that the original MDS rotation is presented and this rotation is arbitrary.) Although the eight scales do not form a perfectly equidistant circle (as predicted by the model), this theoretical ideal is nearly impossible to obtain with actual data. The actual distance between the scales, however, is roughly equal, providing strong support for the model and the assessment of that model. Figure A.6 allows for a visual inspection of the relationships among the DiSC Leadership subscales, which are also arranged in a clear circular pattern.

We were also curious about overall effectiveness. That is, are some of the dimensions of leadership more important than others? Generally speaking, we found that the importance of a leadership dimension often depended on how "effective leadership" was being defined. For example, when we asked which leaders were most respected in their organizations, the Energizing and Deliberate Dimensions seemed to have the most influence. When we asked about the leaders people most enjoyed working with, the Affirming and Inclusive Dimensions had the biggest influence. Overall, however, all of the dimensions had very strong relationships with perceived effectiveness. The lowest correlation with being rated as a good leader was .57 (Humble)

LEADERSHIP SCALES	ALPHA
Pioneering	**.98**
Finding Opportunities	.93
Stretching the Boundaries	.93
Promoting Bold Action	.90
Energizing	**.96**
Showing Enthusiasm	.92
Building Professional Networks	.88
Rallying People to Achieve Goals	.93
Affirming	**.97**
Being Approachable	.91
Acknowledging Contributions	.96
Creating a Positive Environment	.93
Inclusive	**.97**
Staying Open to Input	.94
Showing Diplomacy	.92
Facilitating Dialogue	.92
Humble	**.96**
Maintaining Composure	.95
Showing Modesty	.87
Being Fair-Minded	.93
Deliberate	**.96**
Communicating with Clarity	.94
Promoting Disciplined Analysis	.88
Providing a Sense of Stability	.91
Resolute	**.95**
Setting High Expectations	.91
Speaking Up about Problems	.89
Improving Methods	.91
Commanding	**.96**
Showing Confidence	.89
Taking Charge	.93
Focusing on Results	.90

Table A.2. Leadership Scale Reliabilities

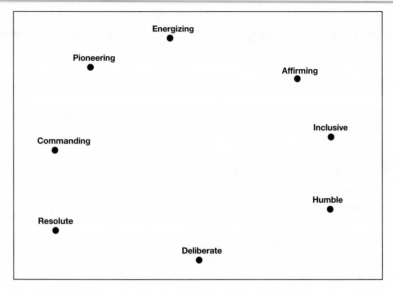

Figure A.5. MDS Analyisis for the DiSC Leadership Scales (The original MDS rotation is presented here. This rotation is arbitrary.)

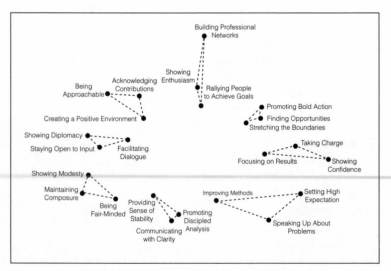

Figure A.6. MDS Analyisis for the DiSC Leadership Subscales

and the highest was .72 (Energizing). These correlations support the conclusion that each of the eight dimensions plays an important role in successful leadership.

As part of our research, we also asked people what they wanted their leaders to do more of. We expected to see a wide range of responses. That is, because leaders are different, with different DiSC styles, we expected that people would ask their leaders for a variety of changes. This is exactly what we found. For instance, people with the D (Commanding) style were most often asked to acknowledge the contributions of others. People with the i (Energizing) style were most often asked to improve methods and processes that their teams use. People with the S (Inclusive) style were most often asked to find more opportunities for their teams. People with the C (Deliberate) style were most often asked to rally the team to achieve their goals.

One of the biggest surprises came as we were conducting the qualitative portion of our research. As part of the study, we interviewed seasoned leaders with different DiSC styles about their experiences and growth as leaders. We expected that leaders would identify their biggest challenges and blind spots as those dimensions that were across the circle from them on the 8 Dimensions of Leadership Model. For instance, we expected that a Resolute leader would identify the Affirming Dimension as the one in which she needed the most growth. Well, that's not what we always found. Although the Resolute leader sometimes saw the need to be more Affirming, many times the leader chose Pioneering or Humble instead. There was some predictability, but it wasn't as high as we expected.

In response to this finding, we had to adjust the way we designed this book. Our original intention was to recommend that leaders work on developing the one, two, or three dimensions that are opposite them on the model. We realize now, however, just how large a role situational factors play in a leader's development. For instance, one of the leaders in our study was very Resolute in his outlook, but he felt the strongest need to work on the Commanding Dimension. Why choose a dimension that was so close to his default setting? Well, he was a young leader in a very hard-charging environment. His first need was to gain credibility and show strength. Similarly, we found that many of the people we talked to had unique situations that called for leadership dimensions that couldn't be predicted by a model.

For this reason, we developed the short survey that you can find at the beginning of Part 3. This is the 8 Dimensions of Leadership Needs Assessment, with questions that have been adapted from our 360° assessment tool. Ultimately, our research has helped us to clarify the interpersonal domain of leadership and, hopefully, helped you get your head around the intimidating diversity of leadership responsibilities. And perhaps more importantly, our qualitative research has led us to conclude that one of the best predictors of leadership growth is, in fact, the desire to grow.

References

Briñol, Pablo, Richard E. Petty, Carmen Valle, Derek D. Rucker, and Alberto Becerra, "The Effects of Message Recipients' Power Before and After Persuasion: A Self-Validation Analysis," *Journal of Personality and Social Psychology* 6 (2007): 1040-1053.

Collins, Jim. *Good to Great: Why Some Companies Make the Leap ... and Others Don't*. New York: HarperCollins Publishers Inc, 2001.

Couppis, Maria H. and Craig H. Kennedy, "The Rewarding Effects of Aggression is Reduced by Nucleus Accumbens Dopamine Receptor Antagonism in Mice," *Psychopharmacology* 197 (2007): 449-456.

Drucker, Peter F. *Management: Tasks, Responsibilities, Practices*. New York: Harper & Row Publishers Inc., 1974.

Drucker, Peter F. Foreword to *The Leader of the Future: New Visions, Strategies, and Practices for the Next Era*, edited by Richard Beckhard, Frances Hesselbein, and Marshall Goldsmith. San Francisco: Jossey-Bass, 1996.

Gaddis, Blaine, Shane Connelly, and Michael D. Mumford, "Failure Feedback as an Affective Event: Influences of Leader Affect on Subordinate Attitudes and Performance," *The Leadership Quarterly* 15 (2004): 663-686.

Galinsky, Adam D., Deborah H. Gruenfeld, and Joe C. Magee, "From Power to Action," *Journal of Personality and Social Psychology* 85 (2003): 453-466.

Gollwitzer, Peter M., Heinz Heckhausan, and Birgit Steller, "Deliberative and Implemental Mindsets: Cognitive Tuning Toward Congruous Thoughts and Information," *Journal of Personality and Social Psychology* 59 (1990): 1119-1127.

Kahneman, Daniel and Amos Tversky, "Prospect Theory: An Analysis of Decision Under Risk," *Econometrica* 47, no. 2 (1979): 263-292.

Marston, William M. *Emotions of Normal People*. Minneapolis: Persona Press, Inc., 1979.

Mio, Jeffery Scott, Ronald E. Riggio, Shana Levin, and Renford Reese, "Presidential Leadership and Charisma: The Effects of Metaphor," *The Leadership Quarterly* 16 (2005): 287-294.

Sy, Thomas, Stéphane Côté, and Richard Saavedra, "The Contagious Leader: Impact of the Leader's Mood on the Mood of Group Members, Group Affective Tone, and Group Processes," *Journal of Applied Psychology* 90, no. 2 (2005): 295-305.

Tetlock, Philip E. *Political Judgment: How Good Is It? How Can We Know?* Princeton: Princeton University Press, 2005.

Westen, Drew, Pavel S. Blagov, Keith Harenski, Clint Kilts, and Stephan Hamann, "Neural Bases of Motivated Reasoning: An fMRI Study of Emotional Constraints on Partisan Political Judgment in the 2004 U.S. Presidential Election," *Journal of Cognitive Neuroscience* 18 (2006): 1947-1958.

Index

About Inscape Publishing

Inscape Publishing, Inc., headquartered in Minneapolis, Minnesota, is a leading developer of DiSC®-based corporate training and assessment solutions. Inscape recently launched Everything DiSC®, its third-generation applications that combine online assessment, classroom facilitation, and post-training follow-up reports to create powerful, personalized workplace development experiences.

With a global network of nearly 1800 independent distributors, Inscape's solution-focused products are used in thousands of organizations, including major government agencies and Fortune 500 companies. Every year, more than a million people worldwide participate in programs that use an Inscape assessment. Inscape products have been translated into 28 different languages and are used in 50 countries.

For more information about Inscape Publishing and Everything DiSC products, visit www.everythingdisc.com.

About the Authors

Jeffrey Sugerman, Ph.D., is the president and CEO of Inscape Publishing, a leading provider of training materials for the corporate market. Sugerman brings 20 years of experience in senior management, marketing, and business development in the technology, training, and publishing industries. He joined Inscape Publishing in 2001 to lead its transformation into an independent company after Carlson Companies sold the Carlson Learning Company to Riverside Company, a New York-based private equity firm.

Sugerman received his Ph.D. in clinical psychology from Washington University in St. Louis and his B.A. from Northwestern University. He was an Assistant Professor at Fairleigh Dickinson University, before joining Sirota and Alper Associates, a consulting firm that provided organizational development consulting services to Fortune 500 companies. Sugerman has worked in corporate publishing since 1988, when he joined a subsidiary of Harcourt Brace Jovanovich. From 1992 to 1999, he served in various senior executive roles in the Assessments Division of National Computer Systems, now a subsidiary of Pearson PLC.

Sugerman is past-President of ISA, the trade association for training and development industry suppliers. He is the 2009 recipient of ISA's prestigious Broomfield Award.

Sugerman currently serves as a Board member for Coffee House Press, an independent, not-for-profit literary press based in Minneapolis. He serves on the Advisory Boards of experiencepoint, a creator of computer-based leadership development simulation systems, and Management Concepts, a leading provider of training services to the federal government. Jeffrey's non-work interests include playing upright bass in a jazz quartet and practicing yoga.

 **Mark Scullard, Ph.D.,** is the director of research at Inscape Publishing. At Inscape, Scullard is responsible for product development, research strategies, and data analysis. He has over a decade of research and data analysis experience developing psychological evaluation tools and methods.

Scullard has provided industrial organizational research and development consultation to a variety of organizations within the Twin Cities area, most recently at Martin-McAllister Consulting Psychologists. Project areas have included a range of topics, such as the development of client satisfaction measures, the design of personnel selection instruments and structured interview protocols, the assessment of employee attitudes and employee performance, the evaluation of personnel selection procedures, validation of psychological instruments, and the development of return on investment calculators. His research has been published in both academic and trade journals, and he has also given research presentations at national and local professional conferences.

Scullard has provided personal and group psychotherapy in a variety of settings. His experience as a therapist includes conducting mental health workshops and seminars. Although he no longer counsels, he is still very passionate about helping people to understand the cognitive and emotional patterns behind their behavior, particularly in the area of leadership.

Scullard received his doctorate in psychology from the University of Minnesota, with a supporting program in statistics. He has also been an instructor at the University of Minnesota. In academia, Scullard's teaching curriculum has included general psychology, experimental psychology and research methods and statistics.

 **Emma Wilhelm, M.S.,** serves as senior writer and product developer at Inscape Publishing. Wilhelm has a passion for product development and human development, so her current role provides the perfect opportunity to develop innovative corporate training and development products that, in turn, help develop people. Her publishing career has included work at several niche publishers, with responsibilities ranging from research, to content development, to acquisitions.

Wilhelm left publishing for several years to pursue a career in collegiate coaching and teaching. She enjoyed her time on small college campuses teaching undergraduate courses, leading cross country and track and field teams, and advising student leadership groups through NCAA and YMCA programs. She coached at St. Olaf College, Smith College, and North Park University, and she served as an instructor at Smith College, North Park University, and the University of Minnesota.

Wilhelm holds a B.A. in English Literature with a Concentration in Media Studies from Carleton College, as well as a M.S. in Exercise and Sport Studies from Smith College. In her graduate studies, she was particularly interested in the sociology of sport and wrote a qualitative thesis, "Competitive Weightlifting for High School Females as a Platform for Identity Formation." When she isn't developing new products for Inscape, she enjoys motherhood, fitness, and writing creative nonfiction.

Berrett–Koehler
Publishers

Berrett-Koehler is an independent publisher dedicated to an ambitious mission: *Creating a World That Works for All*.

We believe that to truly create a better world, action is needed at all levels—individual, organizational, and societal. At the individual level, our publications help people align their lives with their values and with their aspirations for a better world. At the organizational level, our publications promote progressive leadership and management practices, socially responsible approaches to business, and humane and effective organizations. At the societal level, our publications advance social and economic justice, shared prosperity, sustainability, and new solutions to national and global issues.

A major theme of our publications is "Opening Up New Space." Berrett-Koehler titles challenge conventional thinking, introduce new ideas, and foster positive change. Their common quest is changing the underlying beliefs, mindsets, institutions, and structures that keep generating the same cycles of problems, no matter who our leaders are or what improvement programs we adopt.

We strive to practice what we preach—to operate our publishing company in line with the ideas in our books. At the core of our approach is stewardship, which we define as a deep sense of responsibility to administer the company for the benefit of all of our "stakeholder" groups: authors, customers, employees, investors, service providers, and the communities and environment around us.

We are grateful to the thousands of readers, authors, and other friends of the company who consider themselves to be part of the "BK Community." We hope that you, too, will join us in our mission.

A BK Business Book

This book is part of our BK Business series. BK Business titles pioneer new and progressive leadership and management practices in all types of public, private, and nonprofit organizations. They promote socially responsible approaches to business, innovative organizational change methods, and more humane and effective organizations.

Berrett–Koehler
Publishers

A community dedicated to creating
a world that works for all

Visit Our Website: www.bkconnection.com

Read book excerpts, see author videos and Internet movies, read
our authors' blogs, join discussion groups, download book apps, find
out about the BK Affiliate Network, browse subject-area libraries of
books, get special discounts, and more!

Subscribe to Our Free E-Newsletter, the *BK Communiqué*

Be the first to hear about new publications, special discount offers,
exclusive articles, news about bestsellers, and more! Get on the list
for our free e-newsletter by going to **www.bkconnection.com**.

Get Quantity Discounts

Berrett-Koehler books are available at quantity discounts for orders
of ten or more copies. Please call us toll-free at (800) 929-2929 or
email us at bkp.orders@aidcvt.com.

Join the BK Community

BKcommunity.com is a virtual meeting place where people from
around the world can engage with kindred spirits to create a world
that works for all. **BKcommunity.com** members may create their own
profiles, blog, start and participate in forums and discussion groups,
post photos and videos, answer surveys, announce and register for
upcoming events, and chat with others online in real time. Please join
the conversation!